Once compassion is developed,
it naturally opens an inner door,
through which we can communicate
with fellow human beings,
and even other sentient beings,
with ease,
and heart to heart.

—His Holiness the Dalai Lama

Heart

TO

Heart

A Conversation on Love and Hope
for Our Precious Planet

WORDS BY HIS HOLINESS THE DALAI LAMA

ART BY PATRICK MCDONNELL

HarperOne
An Imprint of HarperCollins*Publishers*

Human use, population, and technology
have reached that certain stage where
Mother Earth can no longer tolerate our presence

with silence.

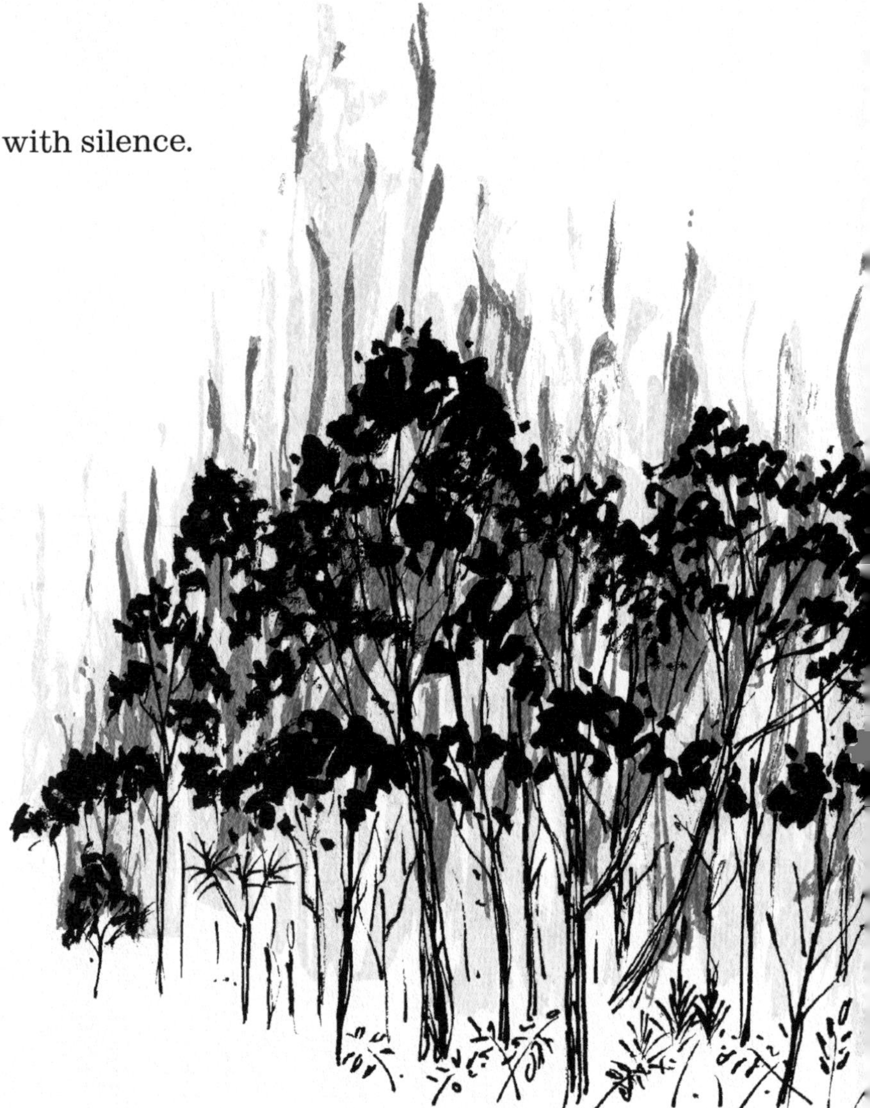

DAINTREE RAINFOREST, AUSTRALIA

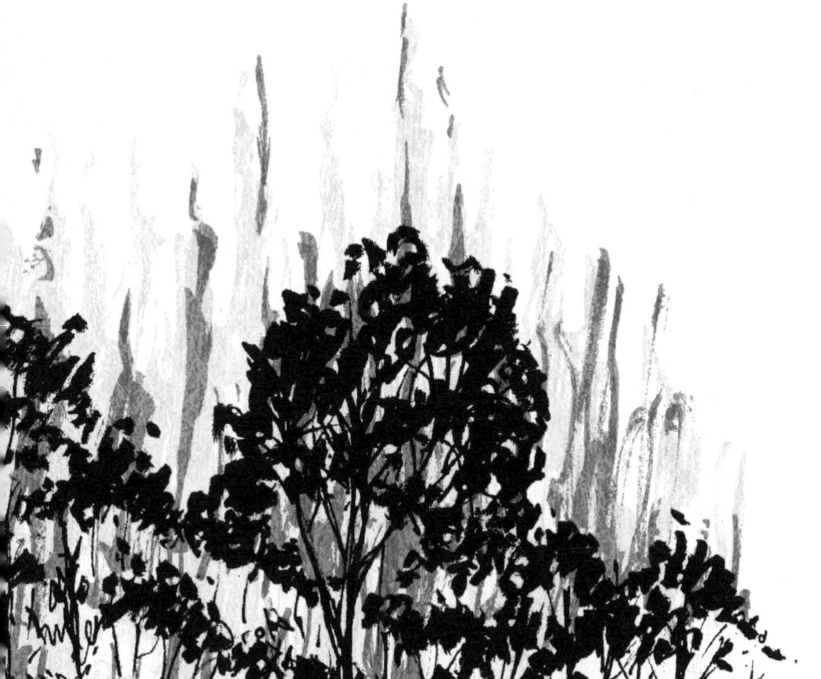

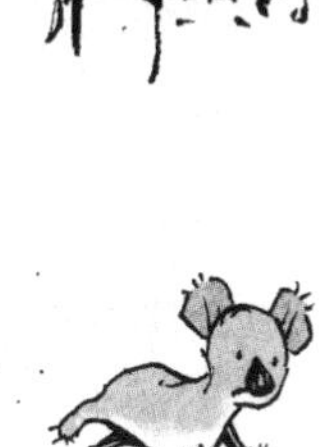

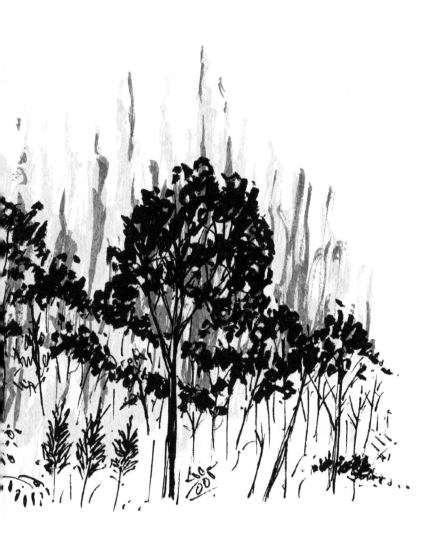

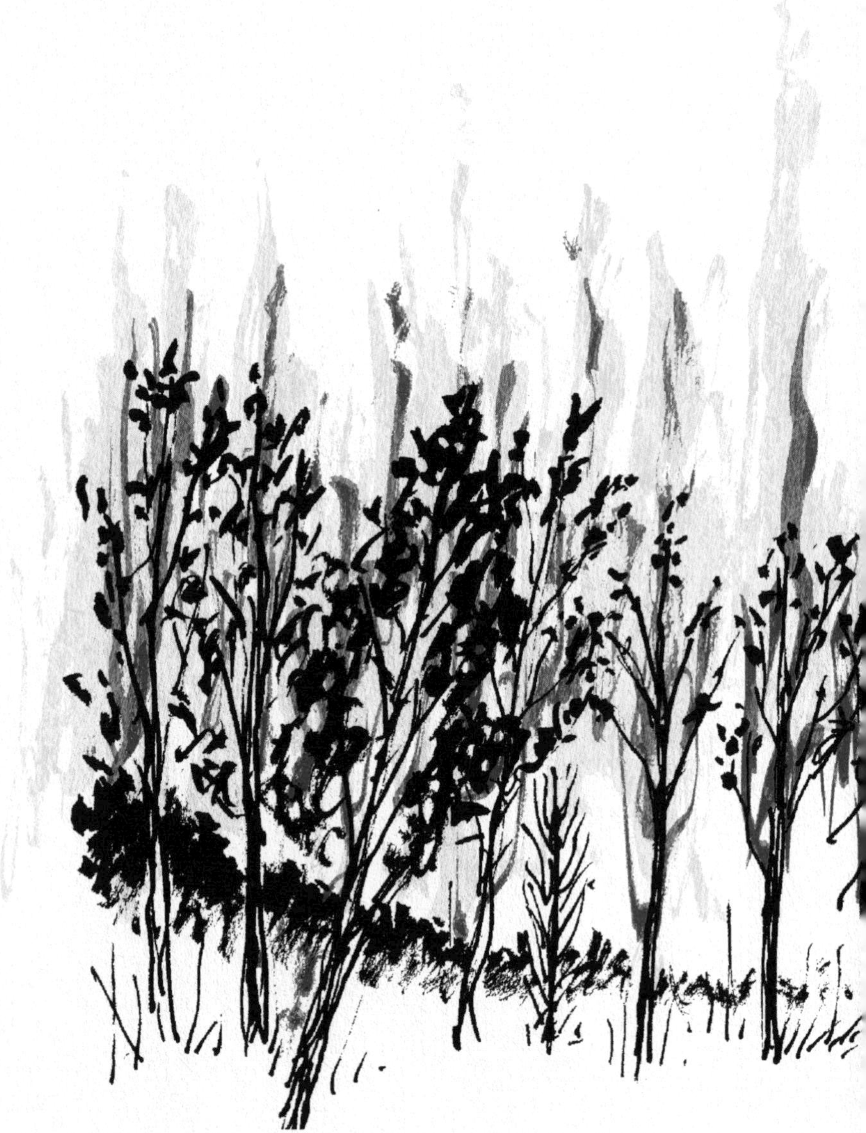

SIERRA NATIONAL FOREST, UNITED STATES

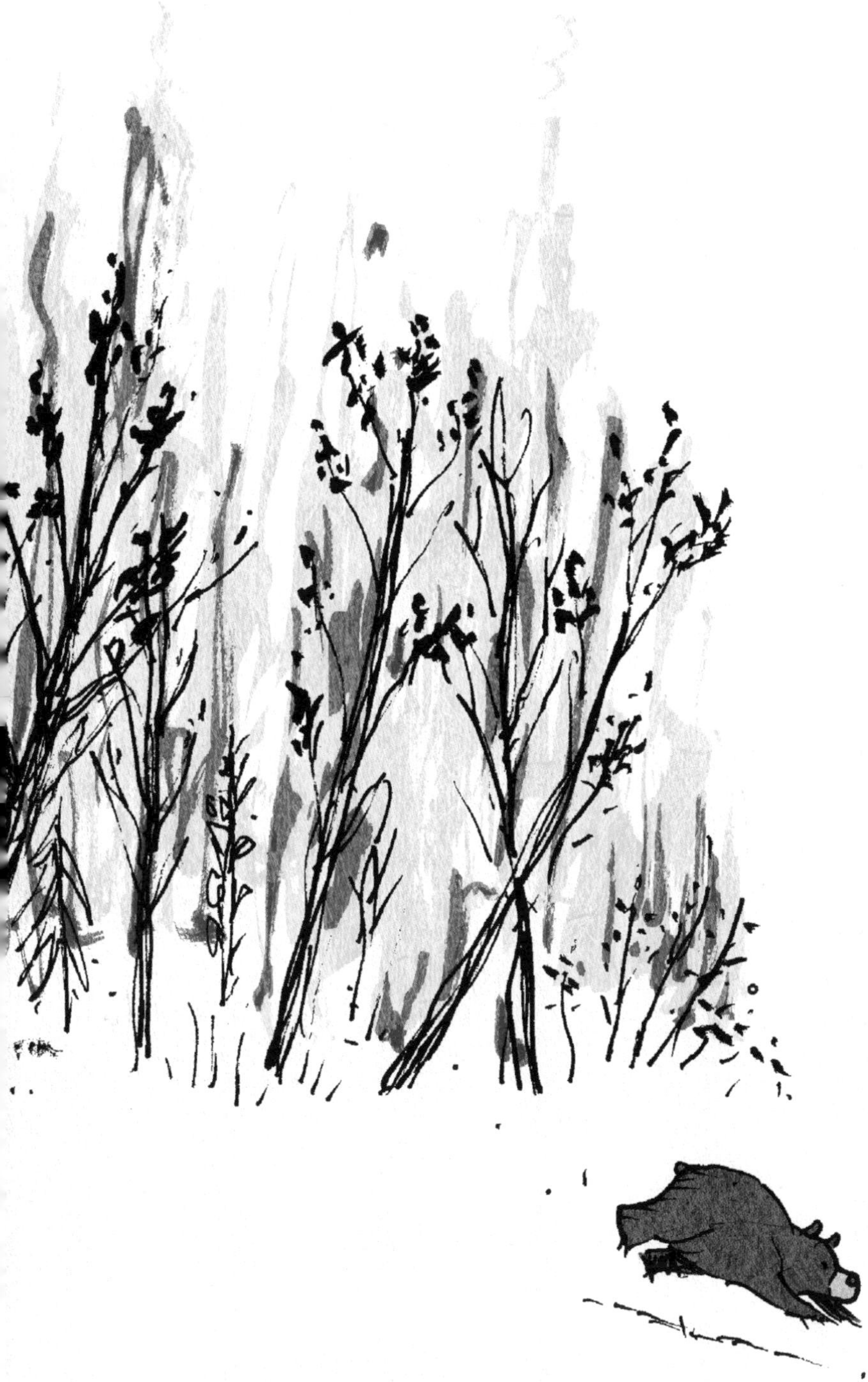

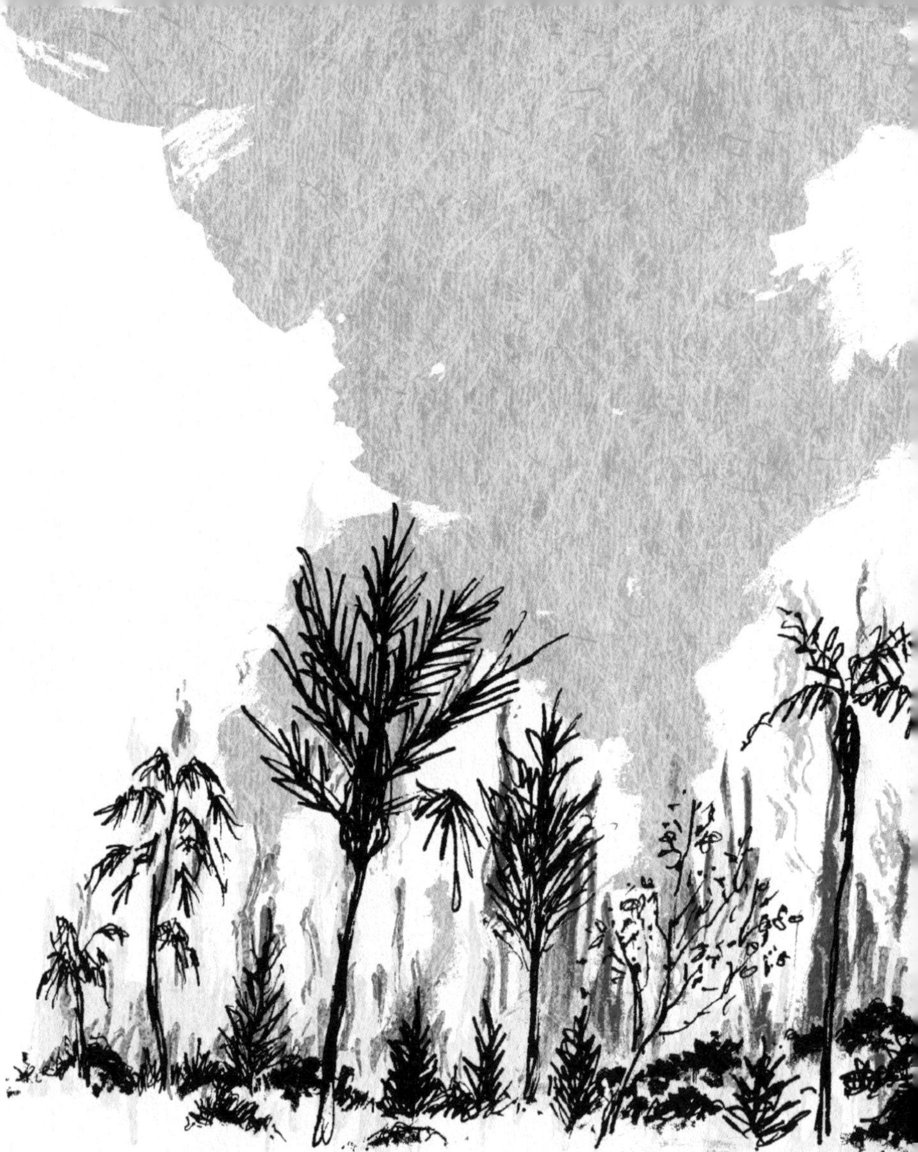

AMAZON RAINFOREST, BRAZIL

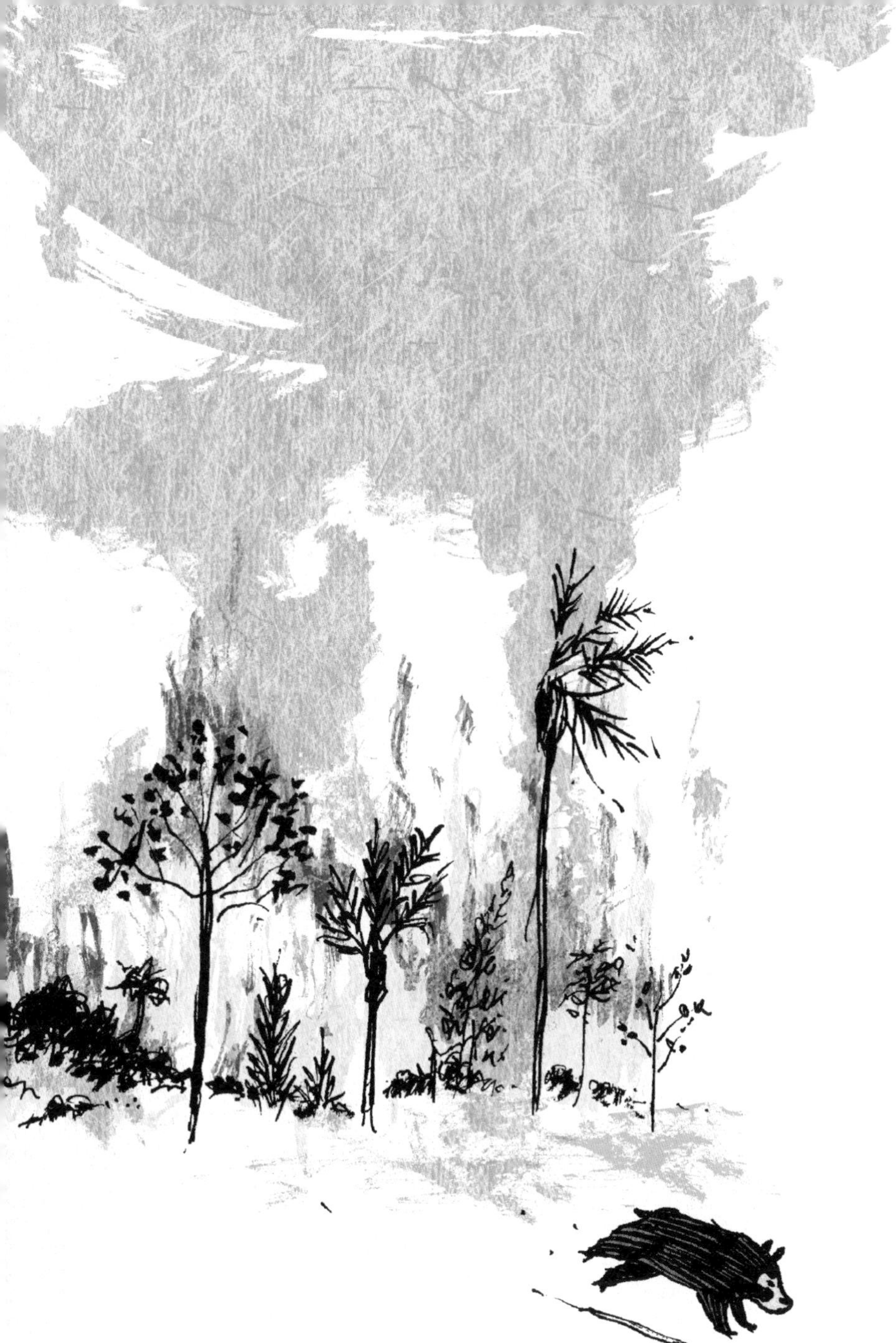

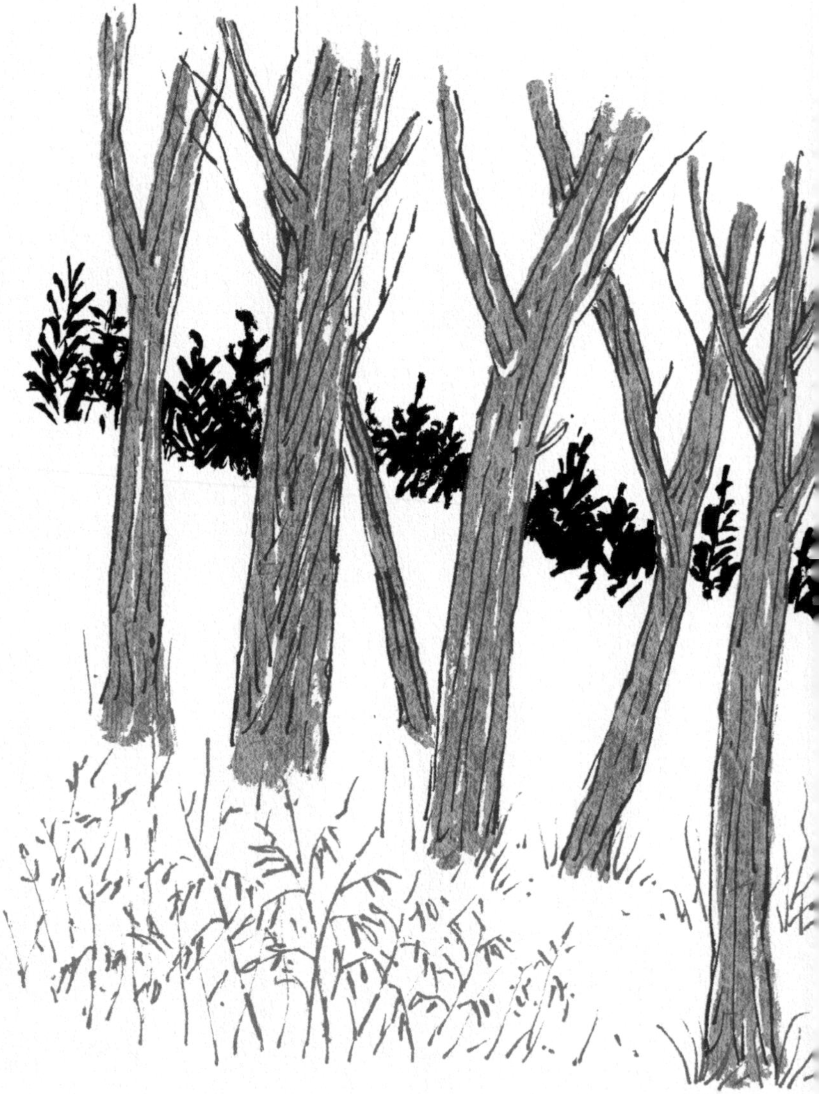

A BAMBOO FOREST, TIBETAN PLATEAU

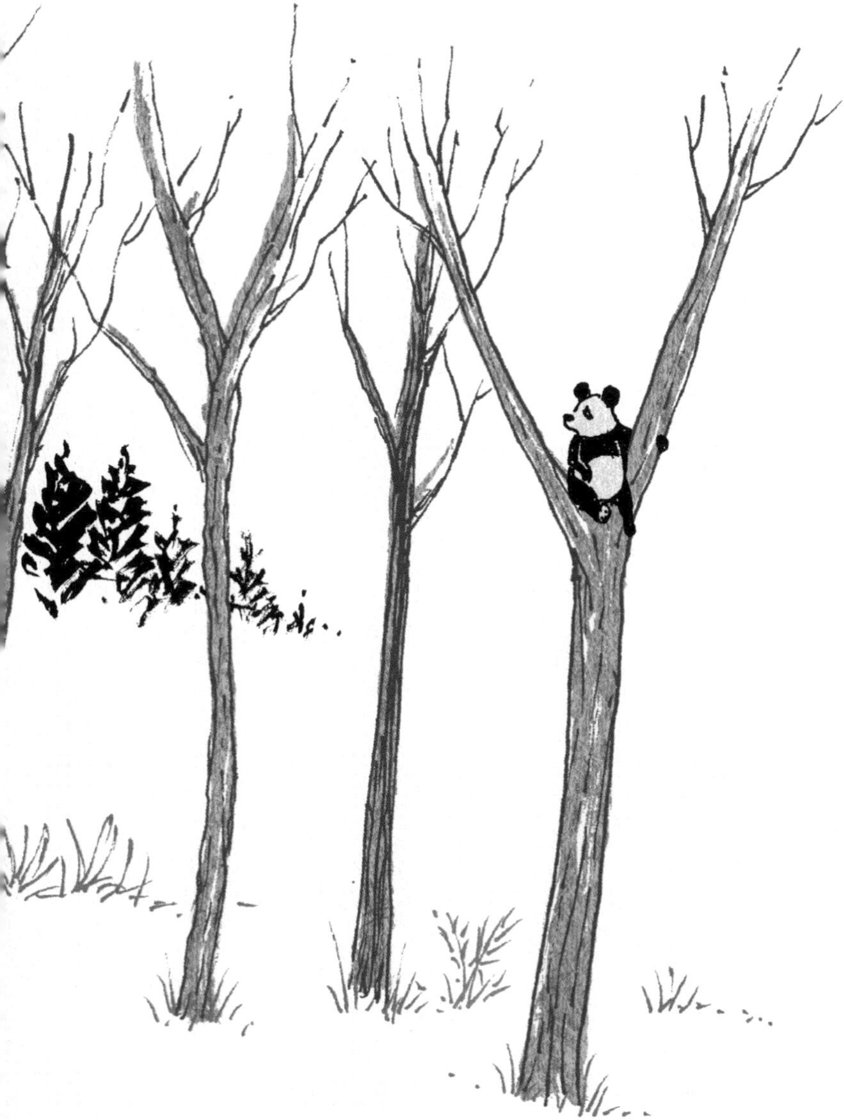

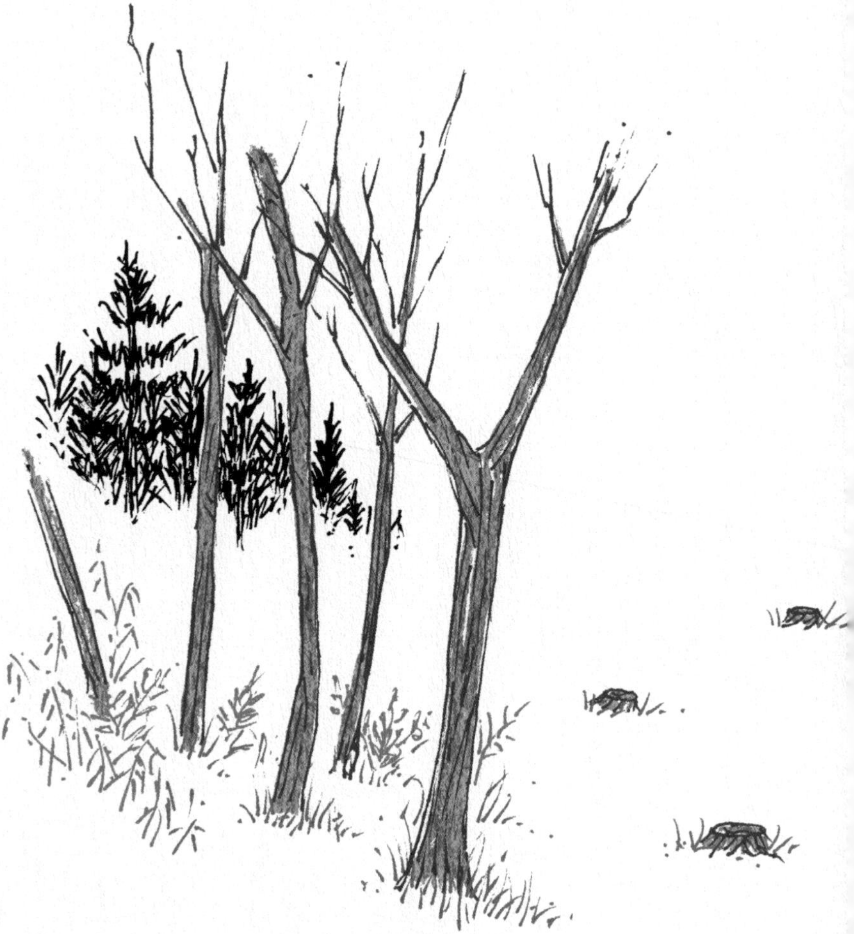

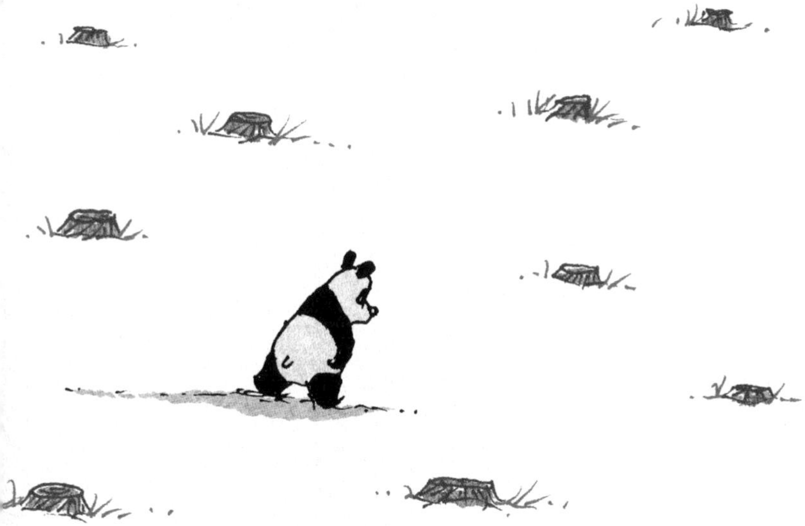

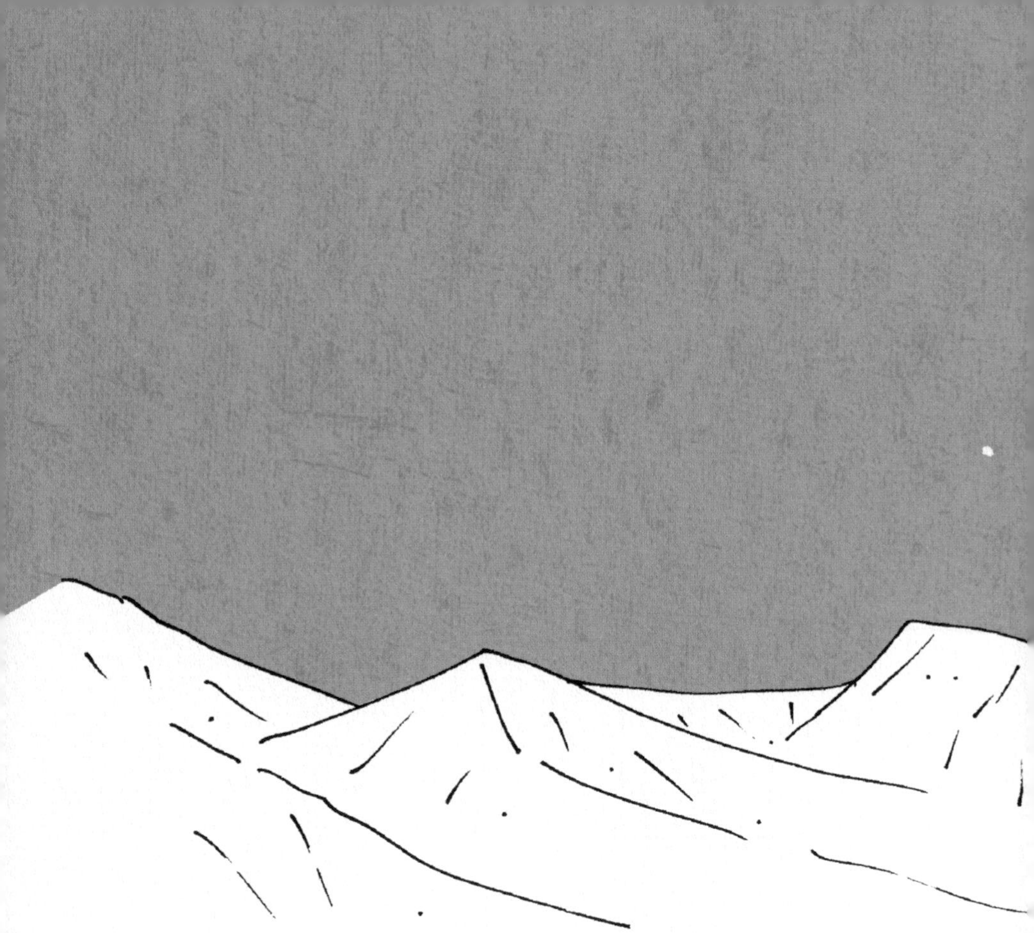

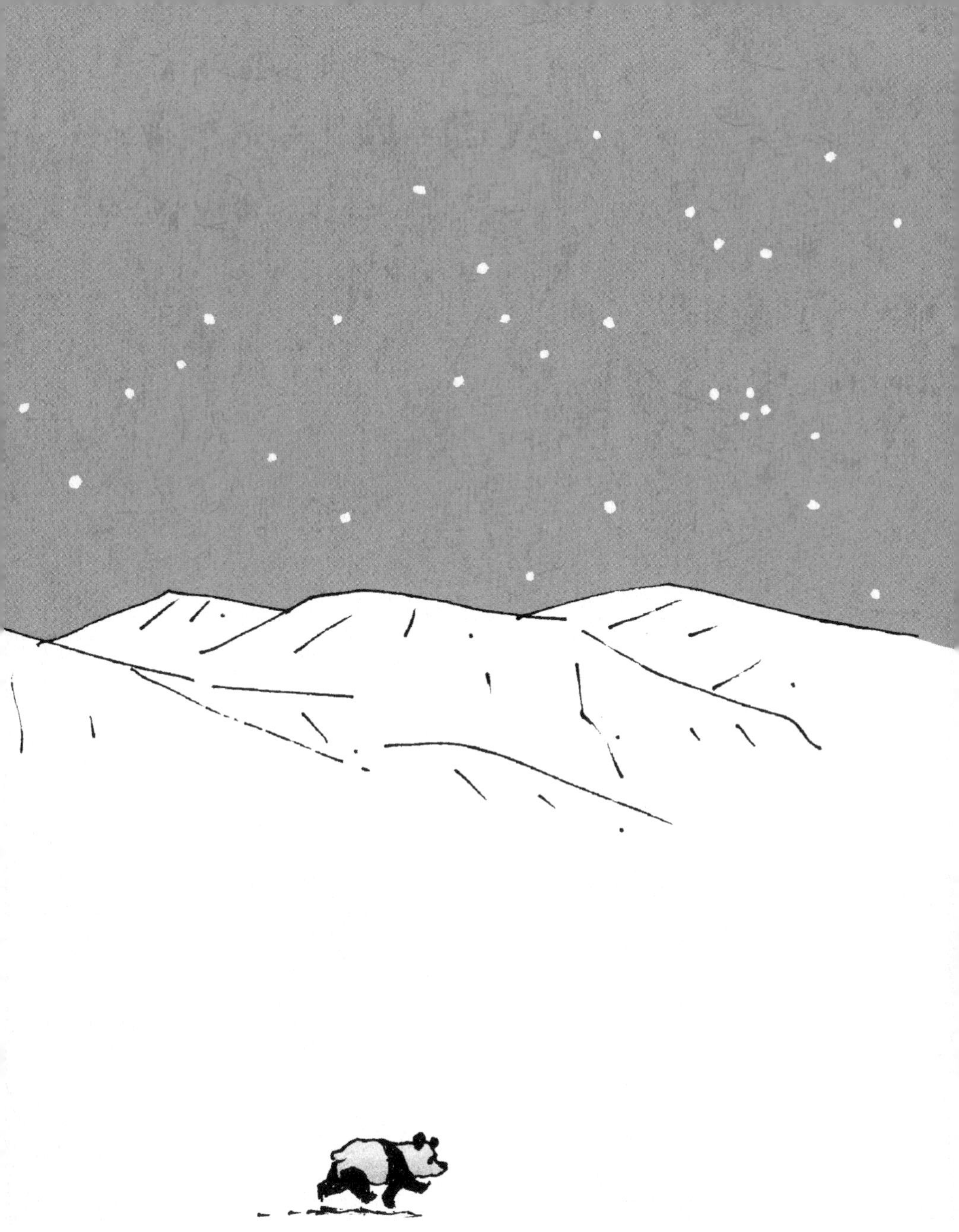

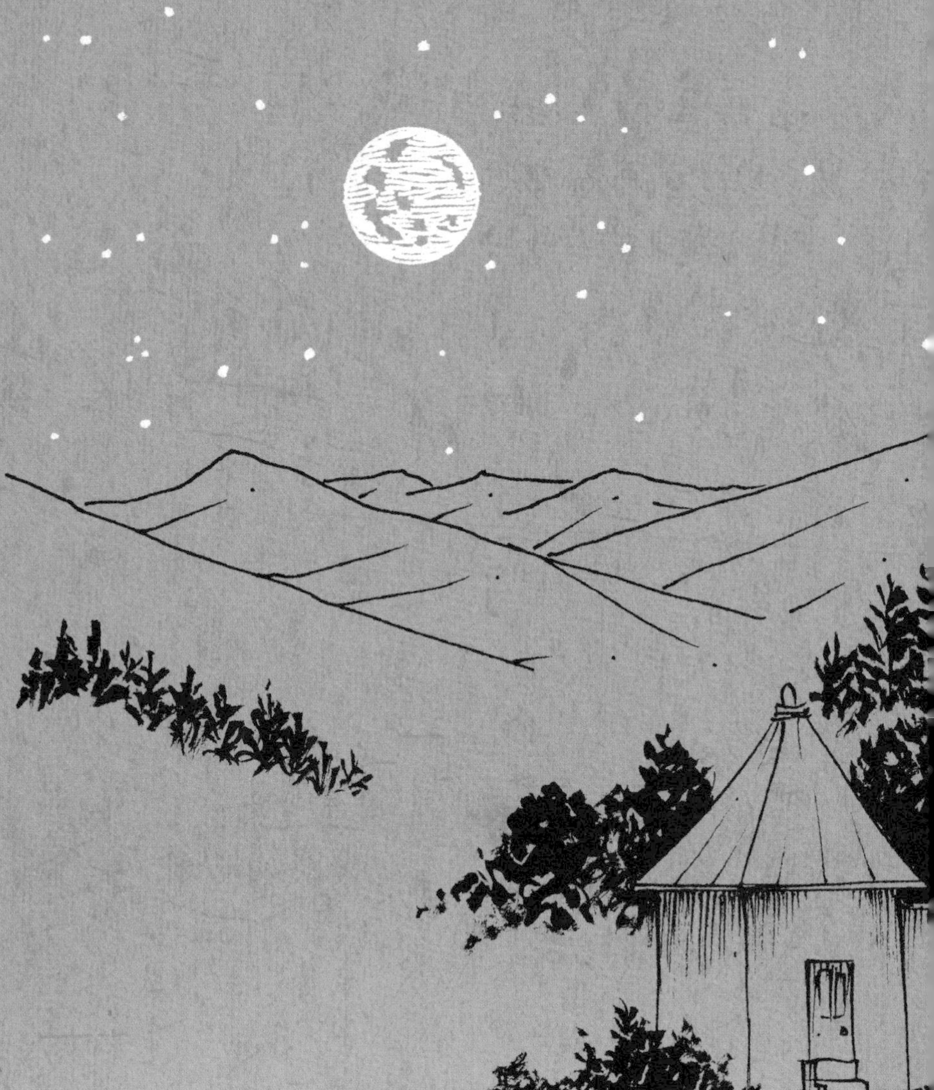

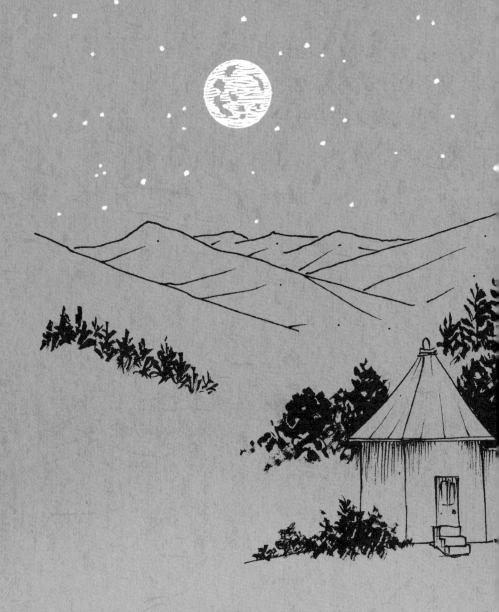

DHARAMSALA, INDIA

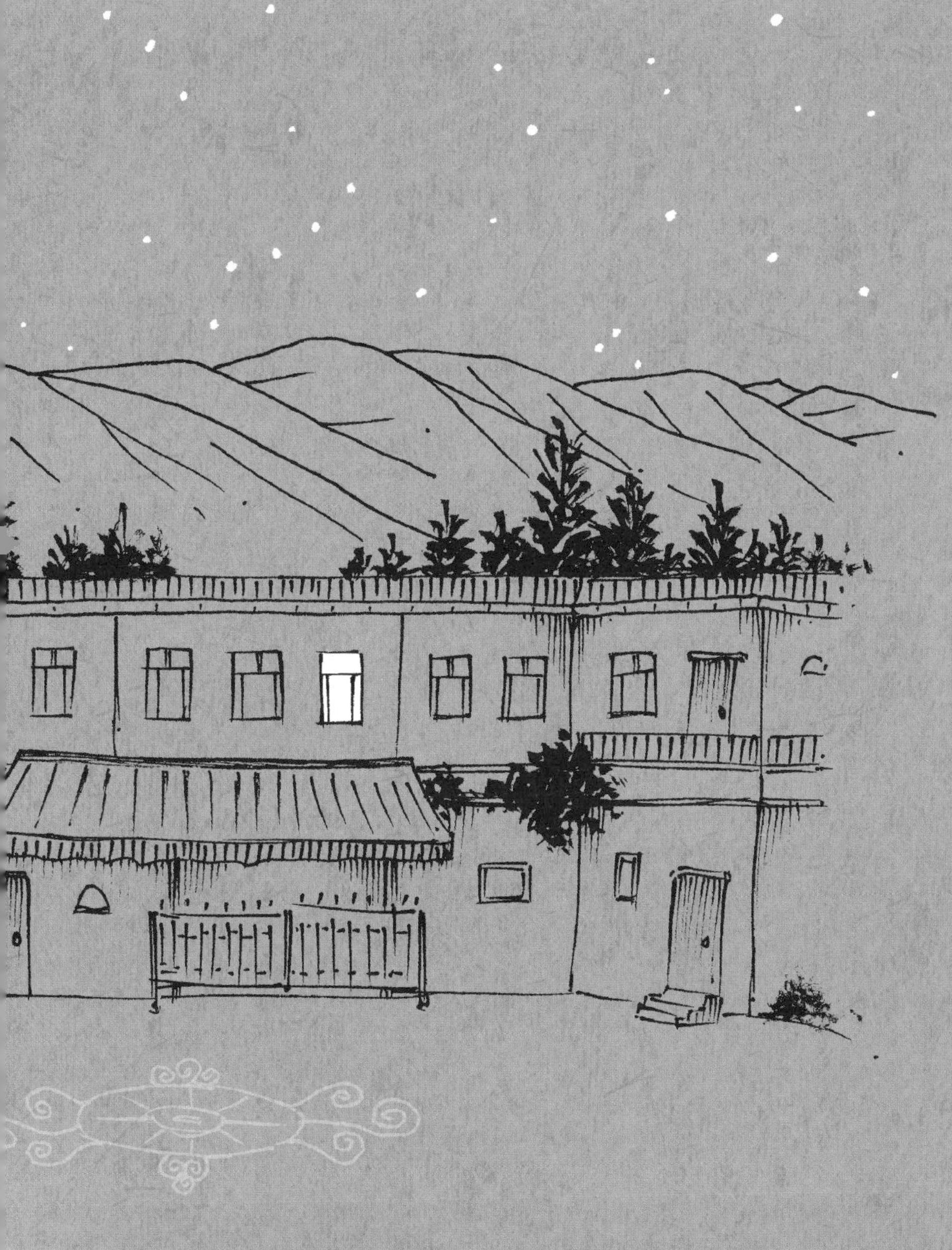

May I become at all times, both now and forever,

A protector for those without protection

A guide for those who have lost their way

A ship for those with oceans to cross

A bridge for those with rivers to cross

A sanctuary for those in danger

A lamp for those without light

A place of refuge for those who lack shelter

And a servant to all in need.

"KNOCK"

"KNOCK"

I welcome everyone as a friend.

In truth, we share the same basic goals:

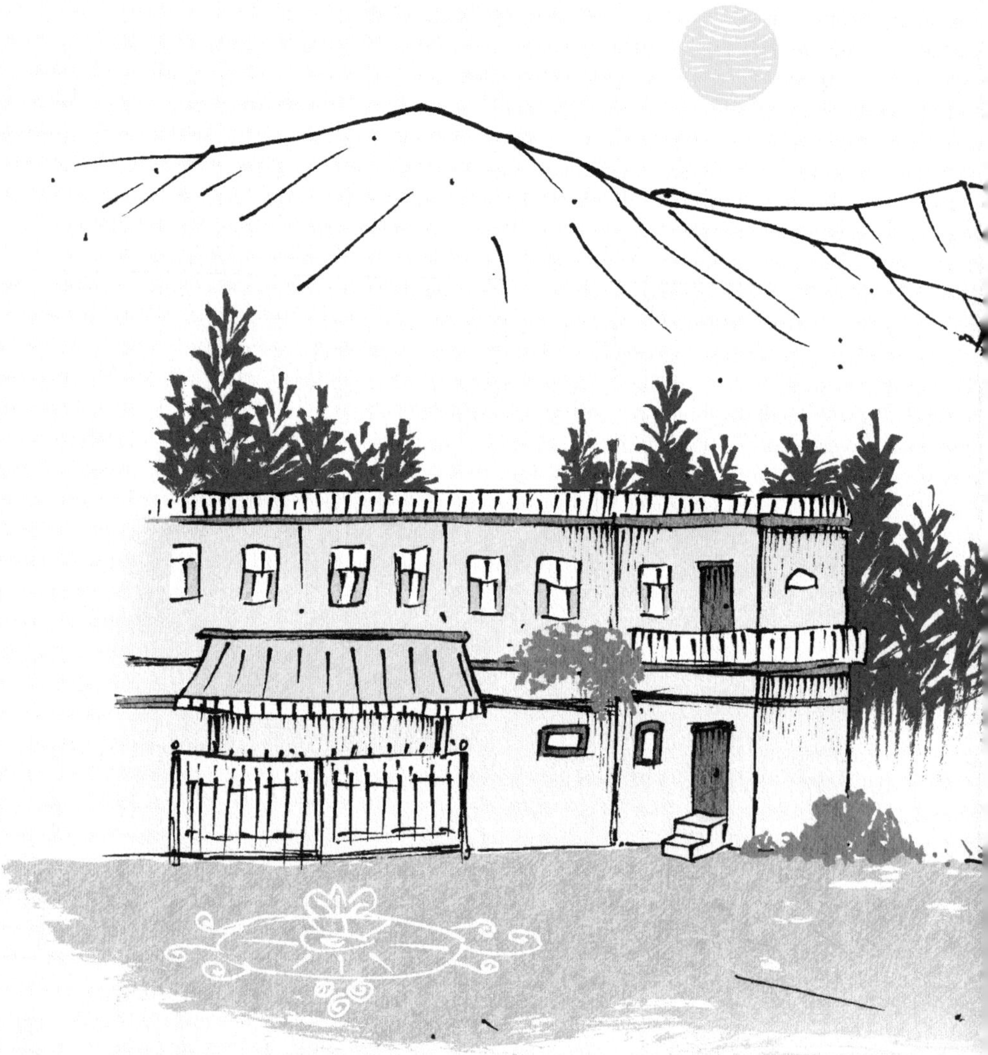

we all seek happiness

and do not want suffering.

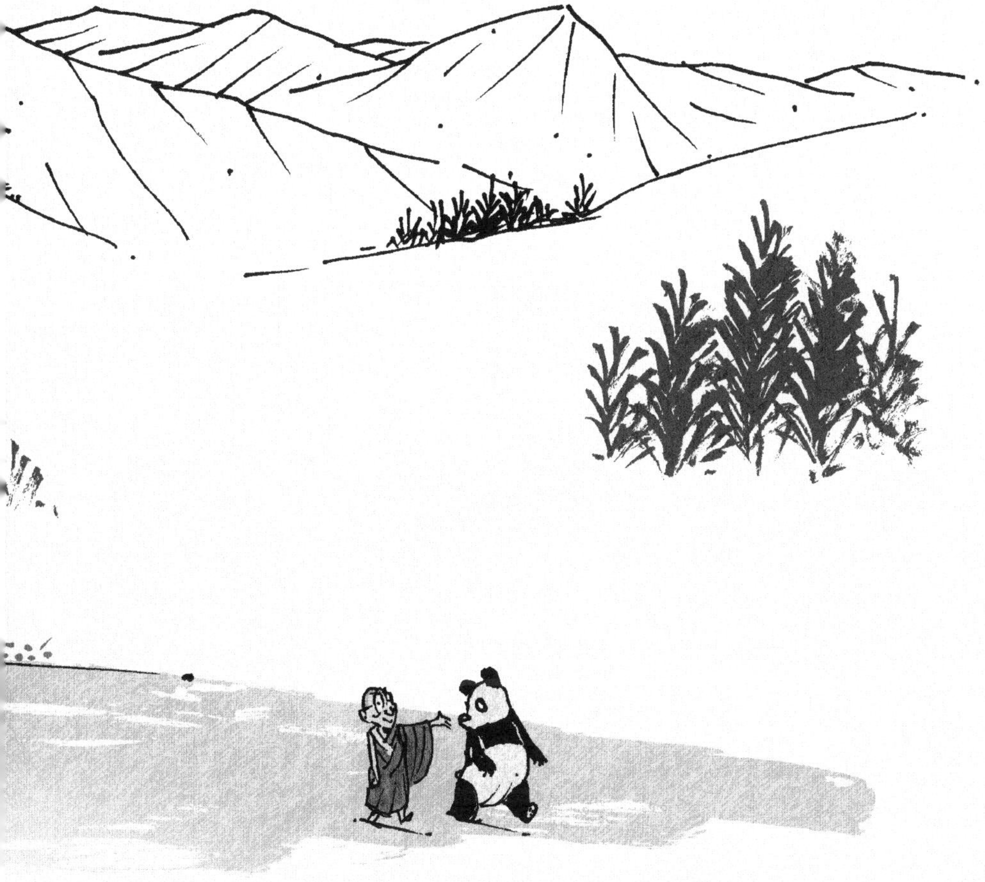

Green forests are nature's great gift.

Forests are good for our soul.

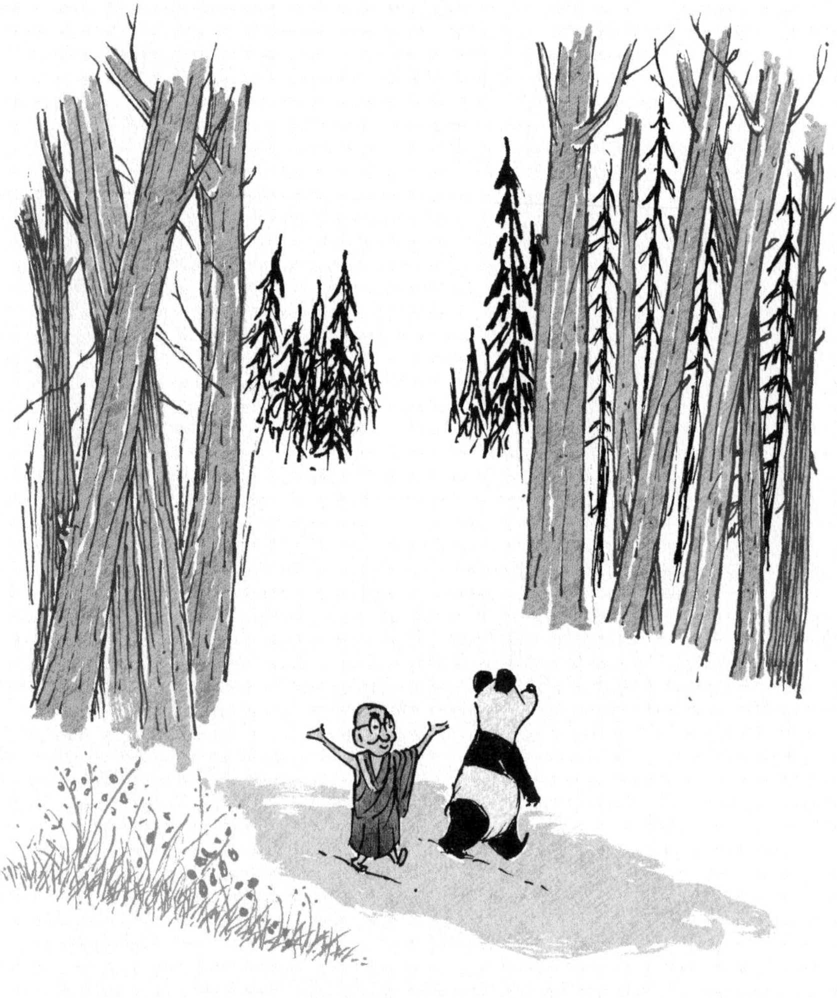

When you spend time in the forest
and hear birds singing,
you feel good inside.

Our relationship with plants and nature is
inextricably very old

and very deep.

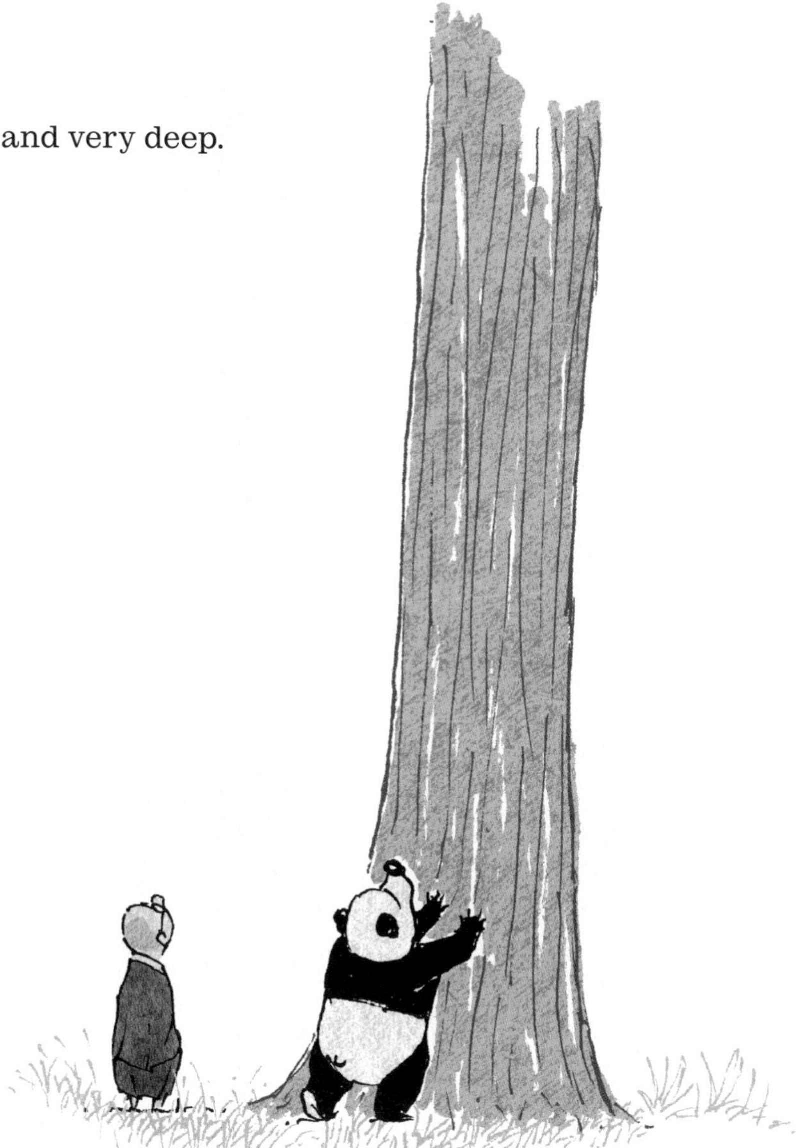

Buddha was born as his mother leaned

against a tree for support.

He attained enlightenment seated

beneath a tree,

and passed away

as trees stood witness overhead.

They say, in the
celestial realms
the trees emanate
the Buddha's blessings.

If I see, smell, or even think about wildflowers,

I feel especially happy.

I remember

when I first arrived in Lhasa as a four-year-old boy,

I felt as though I were in a dream . . .

as if I were in a great park

covered with beautiful flowers

while soft breezes blew across it

and peacocks elegantly danced before me.

There was an unforgettable scent of wildflowers

and freedom and happiness

in the air.

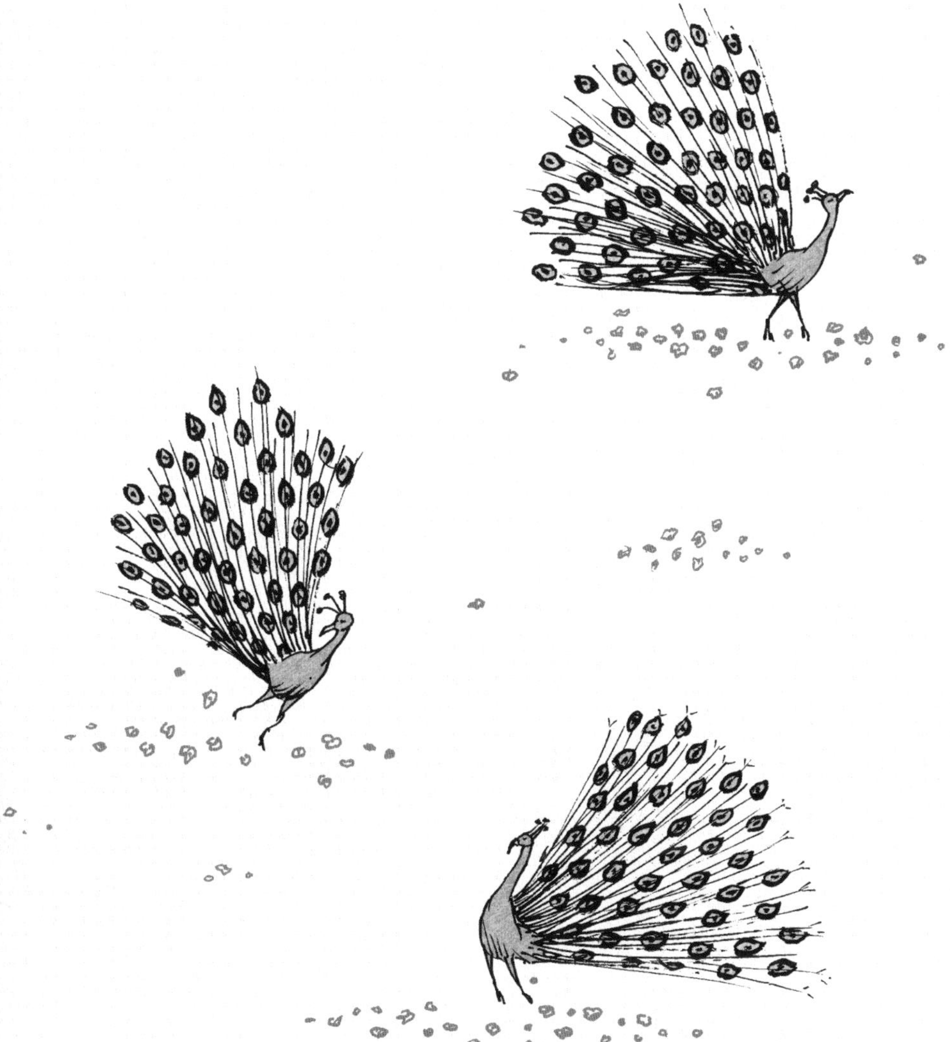

We all feel the need to be surrounded by life.

We need life around us that grows,
flourishes, and thrives.

Because we
all want
to grow,
flourish,
and thrive.

My memory

of the three-month journey across Tibet

from my birthplace at Taktser,

where I was recognized as the Dalai Lama

as a two-year-old boy,

is of the wildlife we encountered along the way.

Immense herds of *kyang* (wild asses)

and *drong* (wild yak)

freely roamed the great plains.

Occasionally we would catch
sight of shimmering herds
of *gowa*,
the shy Tibetan gazelle,

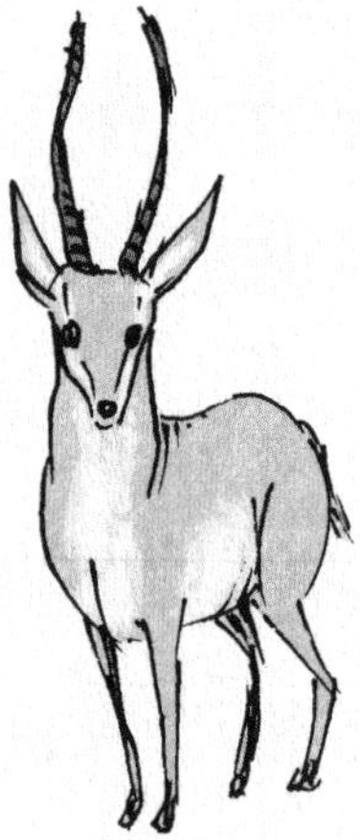

of *nawa*,
the white-lipped deer,

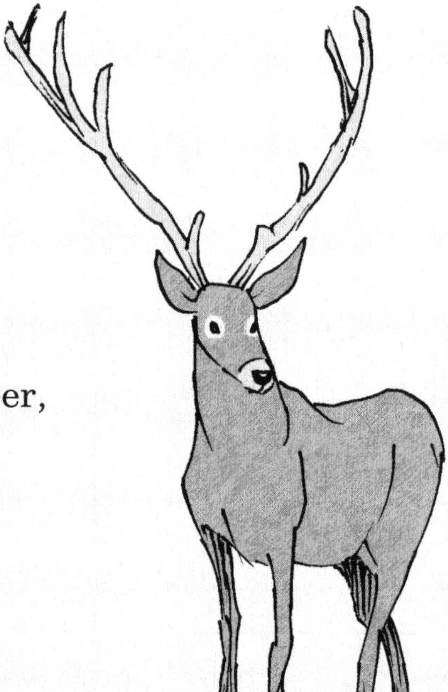

or of *tso*,

our majestic antelope.

I remember, too, my fascination

for the little *chibi*, or pika,

which would congregate on grassy areas.

They were so friendly.

I loved to watch the birds,

the dignified *goe* (the bearded eagle)

soaring high above monasteries

perched up in the mountains,

the flocks of *nangbar* (geese),

and occasionally, at night, to hear the call of the *wookpa* (the long-eared owl).

Even in Lhasa, in my rooms at the top of Potala,

the winter palace of the Dalai Lamas,

I spent countless hours as a child studying

the behavior of the *khyungkar* (red-billed chough),

which nested in the crevices of its walls.

And behind the Norbulingka, the summer palace,
I often saw pairs of *trung trung* (black-necked crane)
that lived in the marshlands there.

Birds which for me are the epitome of elegance
and grace.

And all this is not to mention
the crowning glory of Tibetan fauna:

the *dhom* (bears),

the *wamo* (mountain foxes),

the *chanku* (wolves),

the *sazik* (beautiful snow leopard),

and the *thesik* (lynx),

which struck terror

into the hearts of the nomad farmer,

or the *dhomtra*

(the gentle-faced giant panda).

Sadly,

this profusion of wildlife

is no longer to be found.

"ROAR!"

We must never forget
the suffering humans inflict
on other sentient beings.

Perhaps one day we will kneel down

and ask the animals for forgiveness.

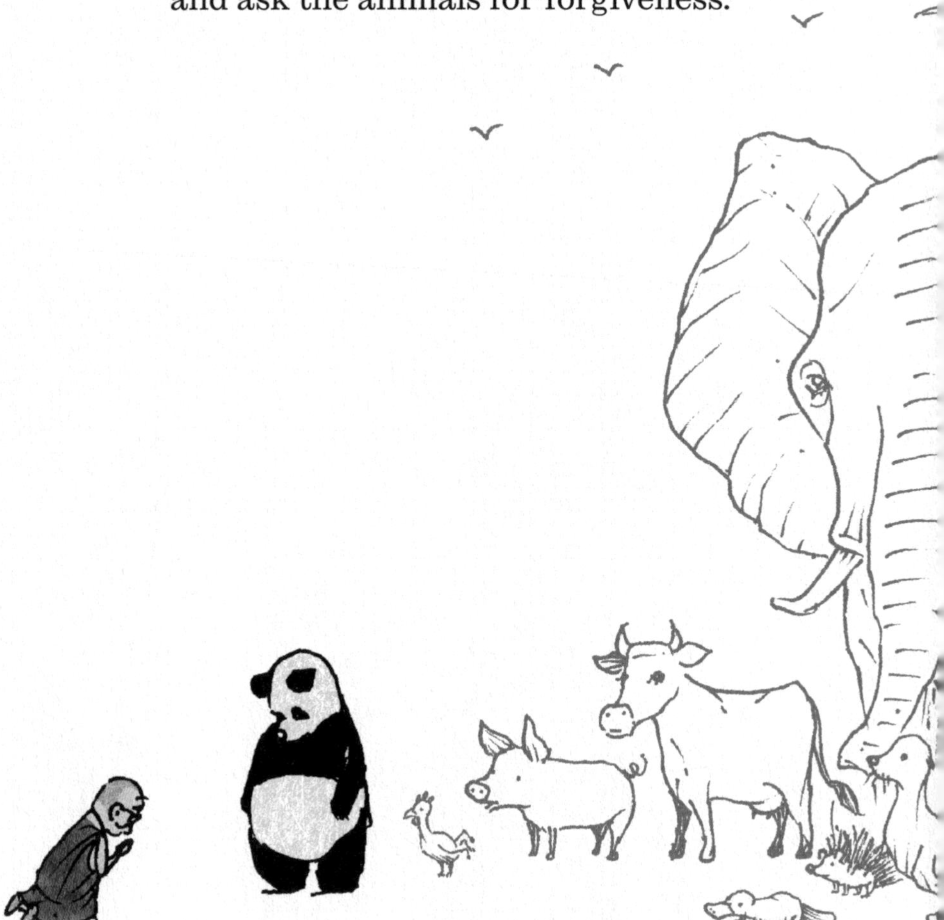

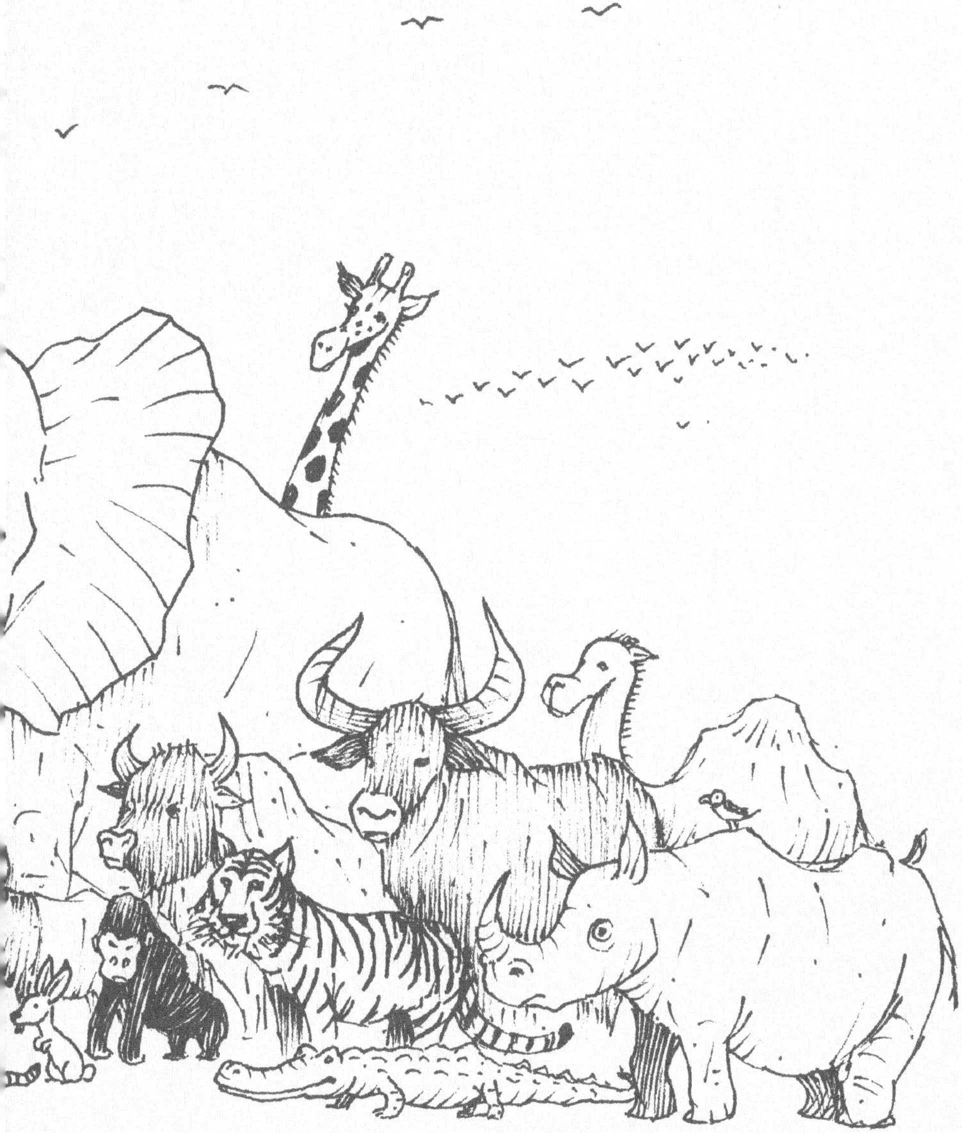

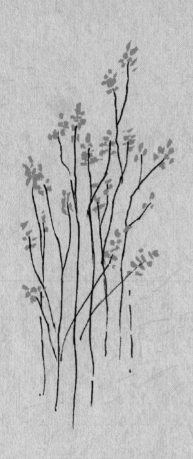

Of all the various species of animals on the planet, human beings are the biggest troublemakers.

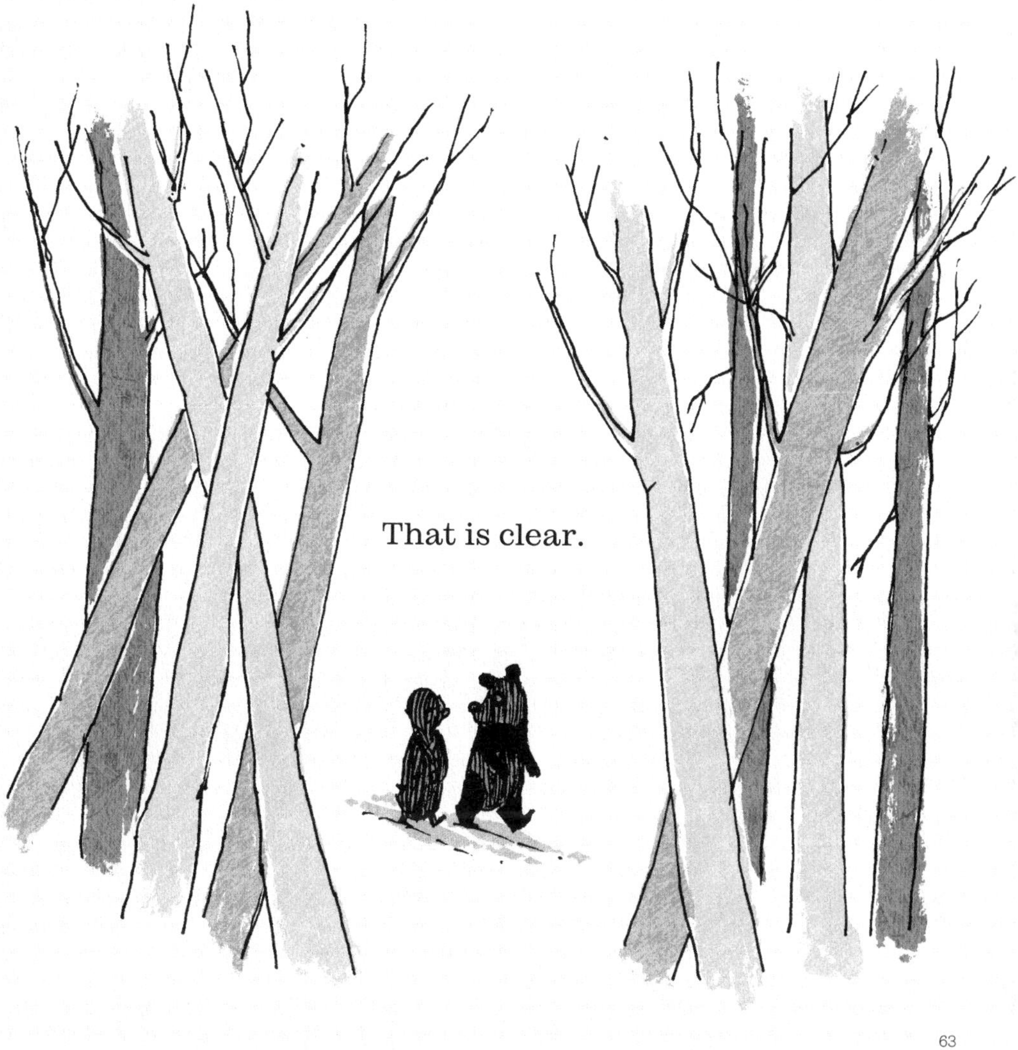

That is clear.

Peace and survival of life on earth as we know it
are threatened by human activities,
which lack a commitment to humanitarian values.

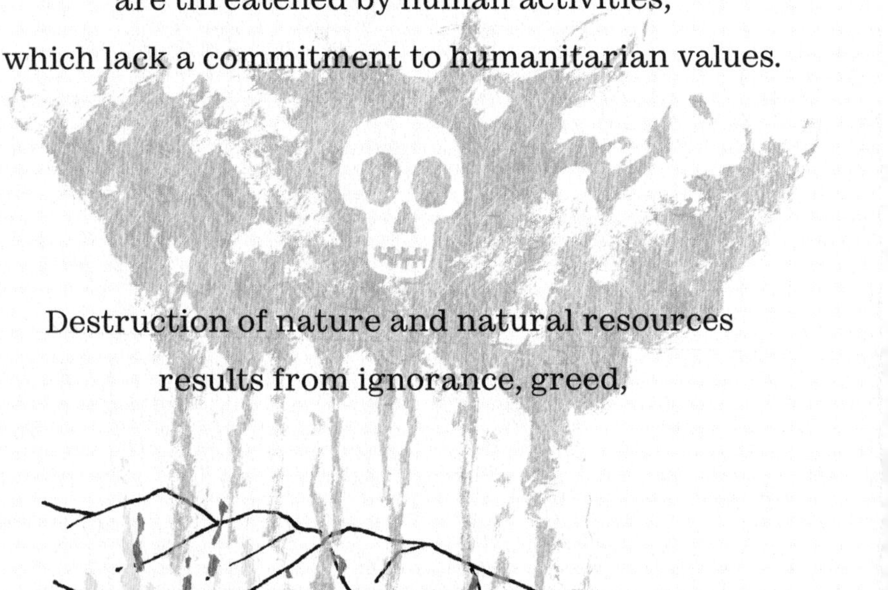

Destruction of nature and natural resources
results from ignorance, greed,

and lack of respect for the earth's living things.

We humans are the only species with the power
to destroy the earth as we know it.

Yet if we have the capacity to destroy the earth,

so, too, do we have the capacity to protect it.

It seems that with development,

the whole world has become much smaller,

but the human consciousness is still lagging behind.

If we want a better future,

we must examine our mindset now.

We need to recognize our nature and then,
if we have the determination,
there is a real possibility of transforming
the human heart.

Compassion, loving-kindness, and altruism
are the keys not only to human development
but also to planetary survival.

Real change in the world will only come
from a change of heart.

What I propose is a

compassionate revolution,

a call for radical reorientation
away from our habitual preoccupation
with self.

It is a call to turn toward the wider community
of beings with whom we are connected,
and for conduct which recognizes others' interests
alongside our own.

I agree with Shantideva when he writes:

Whatever joy there is in this world
All comes from desiring others to be happy,
And whatever suffering there is in this world
All comes from desiring myself to be happy.

One of the most powerful visions
I have experienced
was the first photograph of the earth
from outer space.

The image of a blue planet
floating in deep space,

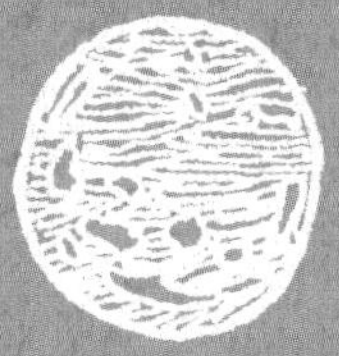

glowing like the full moon on a clear night,
brought home powerfully to me the recognition
that we are indeed all members of a single family
sharing one little house.

This beautiful blue planet is our only home.

What happens on it affects us all.

We have to learn to live in harmony

and peace with each other

and with nature.

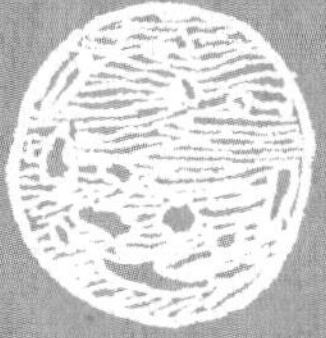

This is not just a dream,
but a necessity.
If we do not look after this home,
what else are we responsible to do
on this earth?

Everything is interdependent,
everything is inseparable.

Our individual well-being is intimately connected
both with that of all others
and with the environment within which we live.

Our every action,

our every deed, word, and thought,

no matter how slight

or inconsequential it may seem,

has an implication not only for ourselves

but for all others, too.

We are all interconnected in the universe,

and from this, universal responsibility arises.

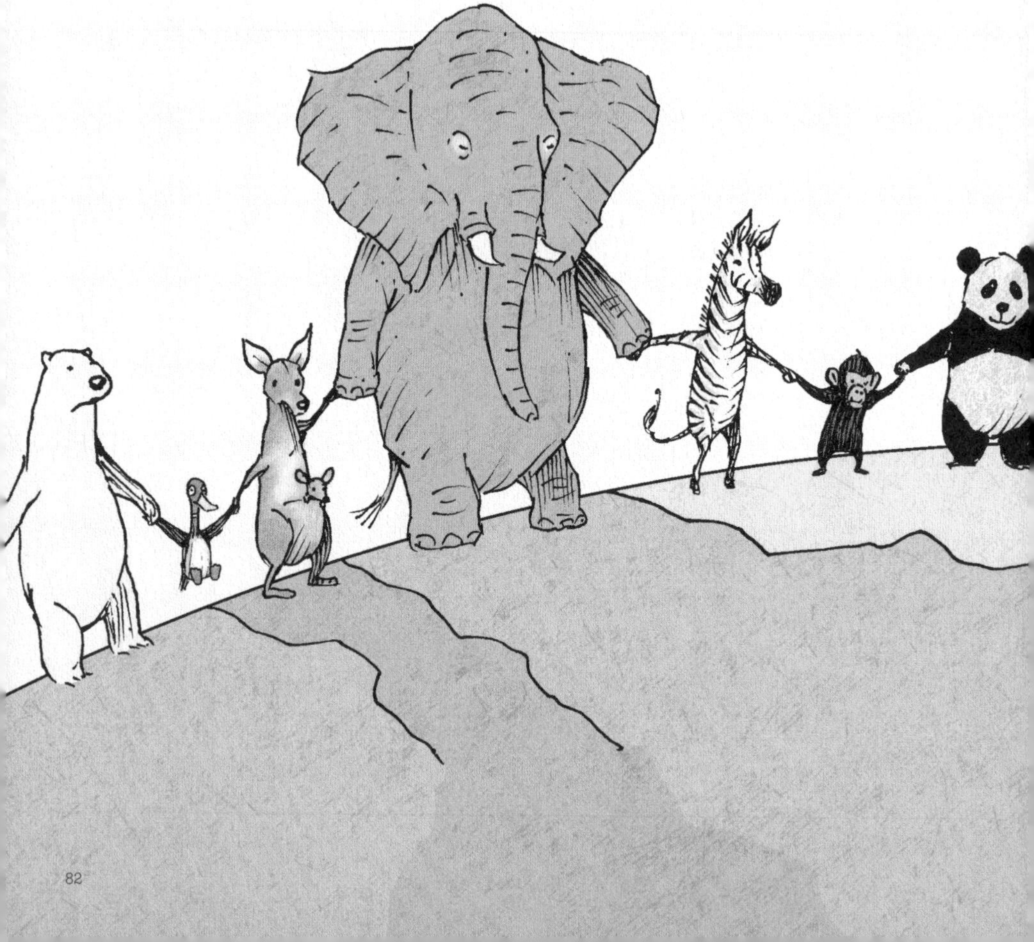

The creatures that inhabit this earth—
be they human beings or animals—
are here to contribute,
each in its own particular way,
to the beauty and prosperity of the world.

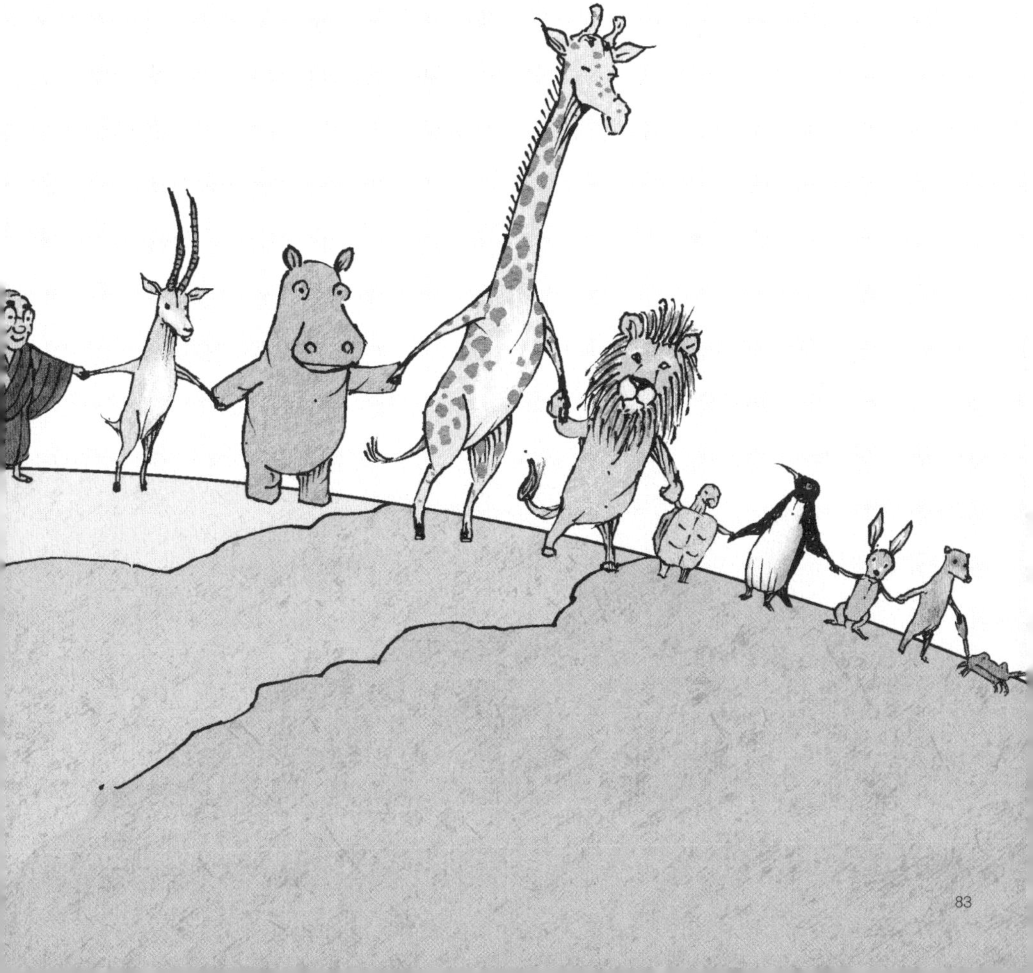

I believe everyone has the responsibility
to develop a happier world.
We need, ultimately, to have a greater concern
for others' well-being.

In other words, *kindness* or *compassion*,
which is lacking now.

We must pay more attention to our inner values.

Develop a sense of oneness of humanity.

If you want to change the world, first try
to improve, change, within yourself.

Creating a more peaceful world requires

a peaceful mind and a peaceful heart.

A good heart is the source
of all happiness and joy,
and we can all be
warmhearted
if we make an effort.

But better still is to have *bodhichitta,*
which is a good heart imbued with wisdom.

We need to cultivate a compassion

that is powerful enough to make us feel committed

to bringing about the well-being of others,

so that we are actually willing

to shoulder the responsibility

for making this happen.

In Tibetan, such compassion is called

nying je chenpo,

literally

"great compassion."

Through developing
an attitude of responsibility toward others,
we can begin to create the kinder,
more compassionate world
we all dream of.

The most important thing is in our mind, here, now,
and the way we use that mind in daily life.

Eliminate thoughts that bring you the uneasiness
and discomfort that come from a negative mind,
from negative thoughts.

Consider whether they are useful or not useful
for humanity and the health of our planet.

If you want others to be happy,

practice compassion.

If you want to be happy,
practice compassion.

This is my simple religion.

There is no need for temples,

no need for complicated philosophy.

My philosophy is . . .

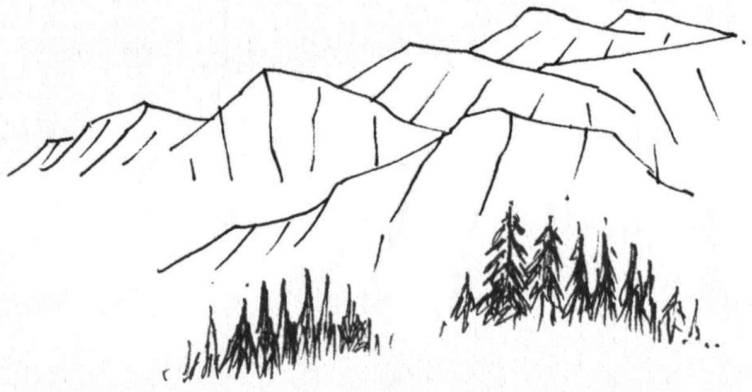

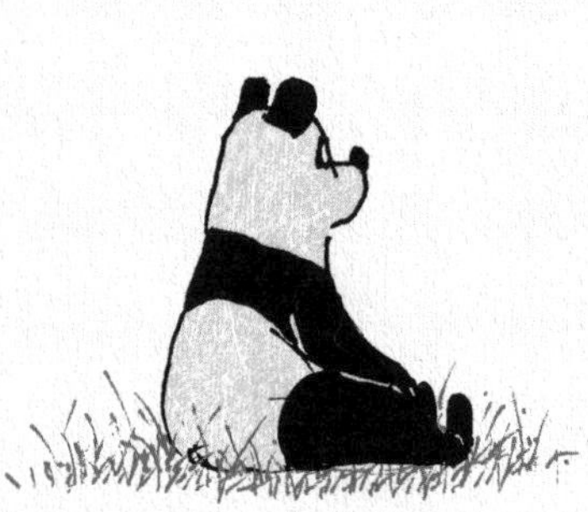

Be kind whenever *possible*.
It is always *possible*.

Compassion is the radicalism of our time.

Consider all sentient beings

dear as your mother.

To some, advocating this ideal
of unconditional love is unrealistic.

I urge them to experiment with it nonetheless.

They will discover that when we reach

beyond the confines of narrow self-interest,

our hearts become filled with strength.

Peace and joy become our constant companion.

It breaks down barriers of every kind

and in the end destroys the notion

of my interest

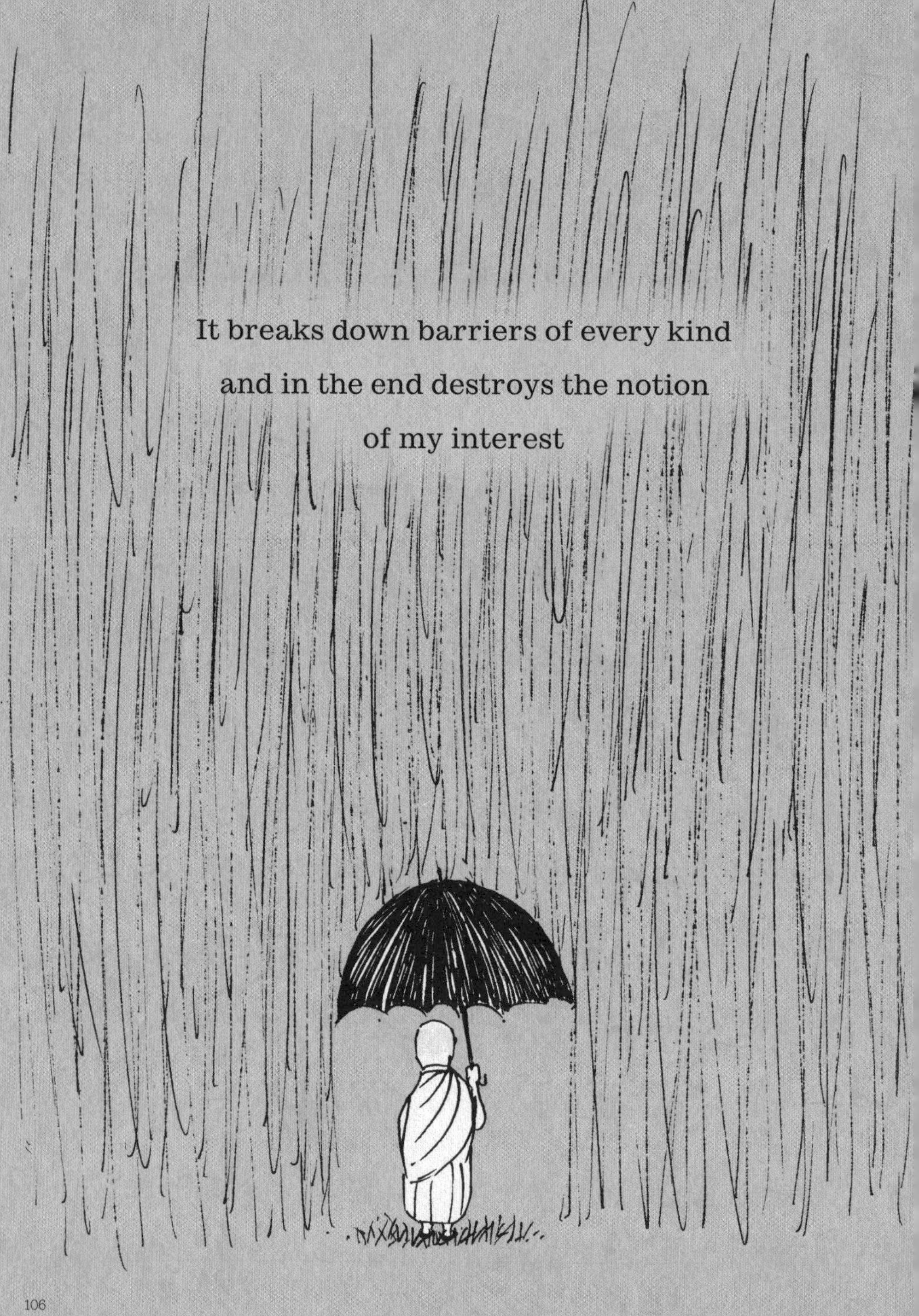

as independent from others' interest.

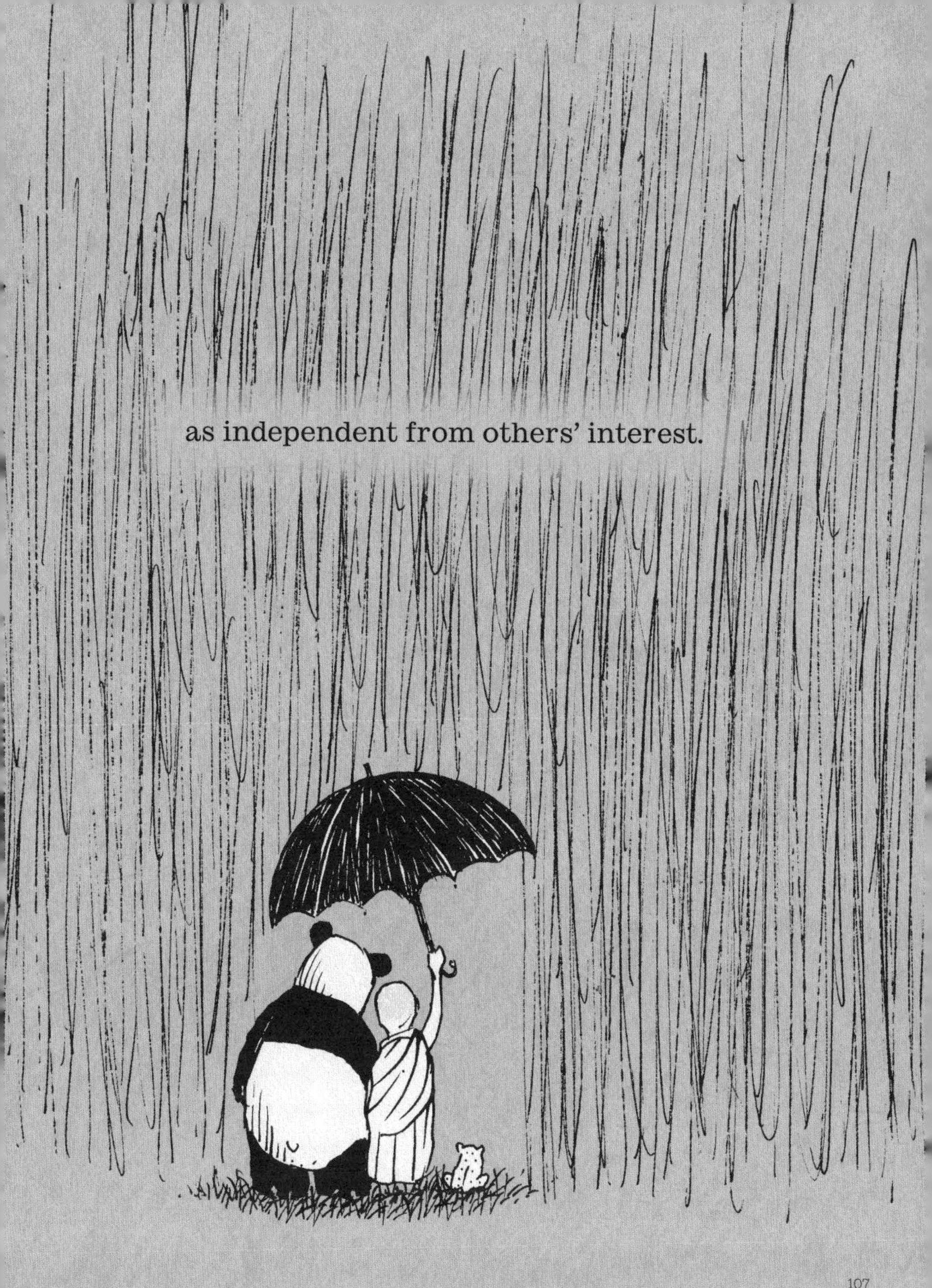

Where love, affection, kindness,

and compassion live,

ethically wholesome actions

arise naturally.

Everything we do has some effect—
even a simple act.

Although it might seem insignificant,

when we multiply it by billions of others

who might do the same thing,

we can have an enormous impact.

Ultimately each individual

has responsibility to help guide our global family

in the right direction.

Good wishes alone are not enough;

we have to assume

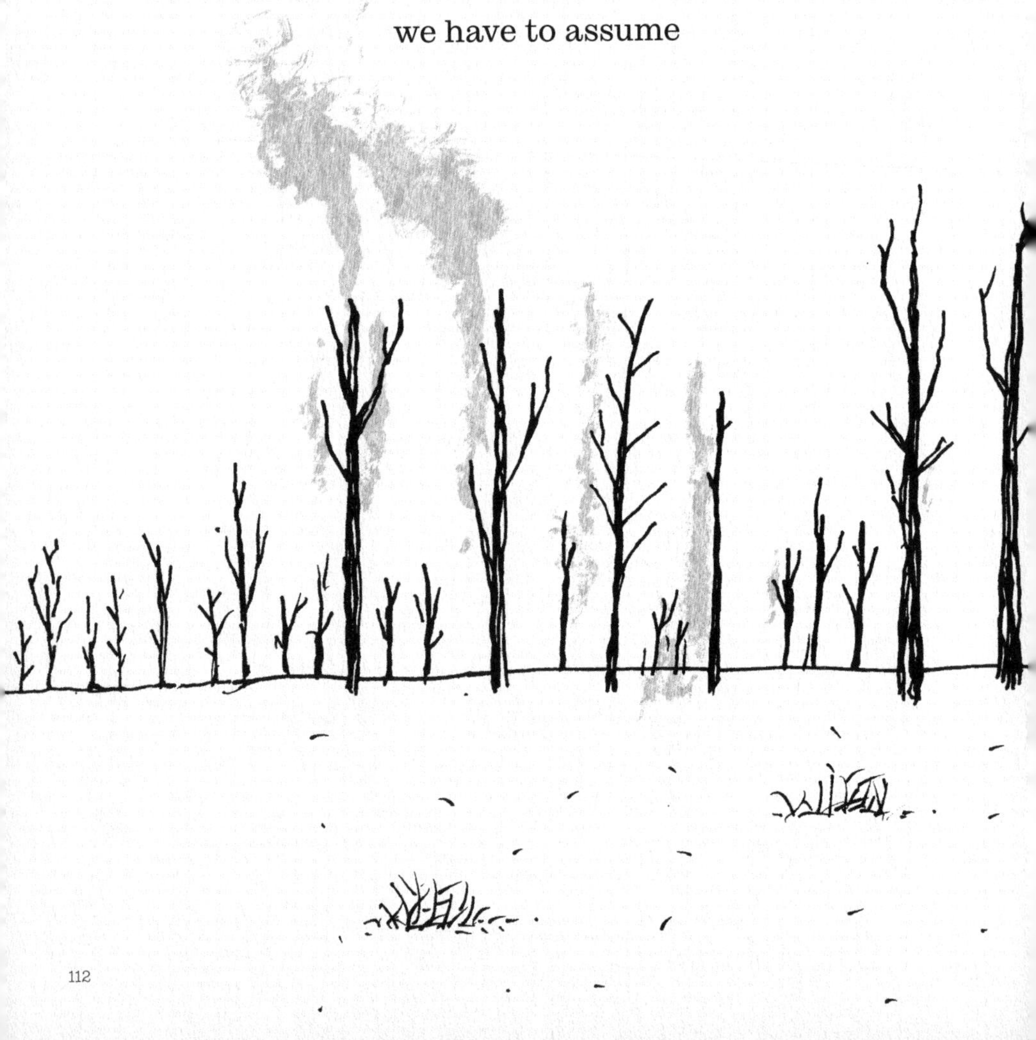

responsibility.

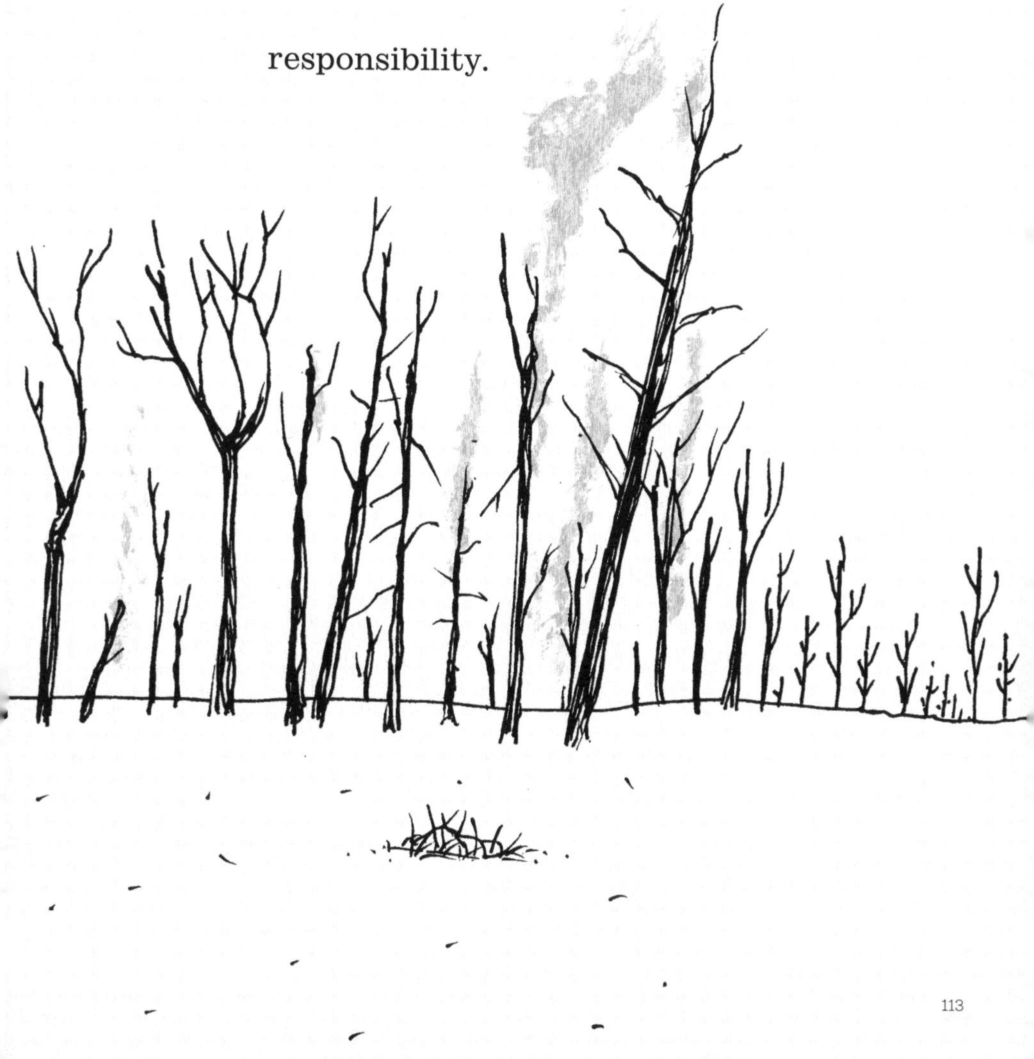

So there is hope for a better future.

It depends entirely on our actions (karma).

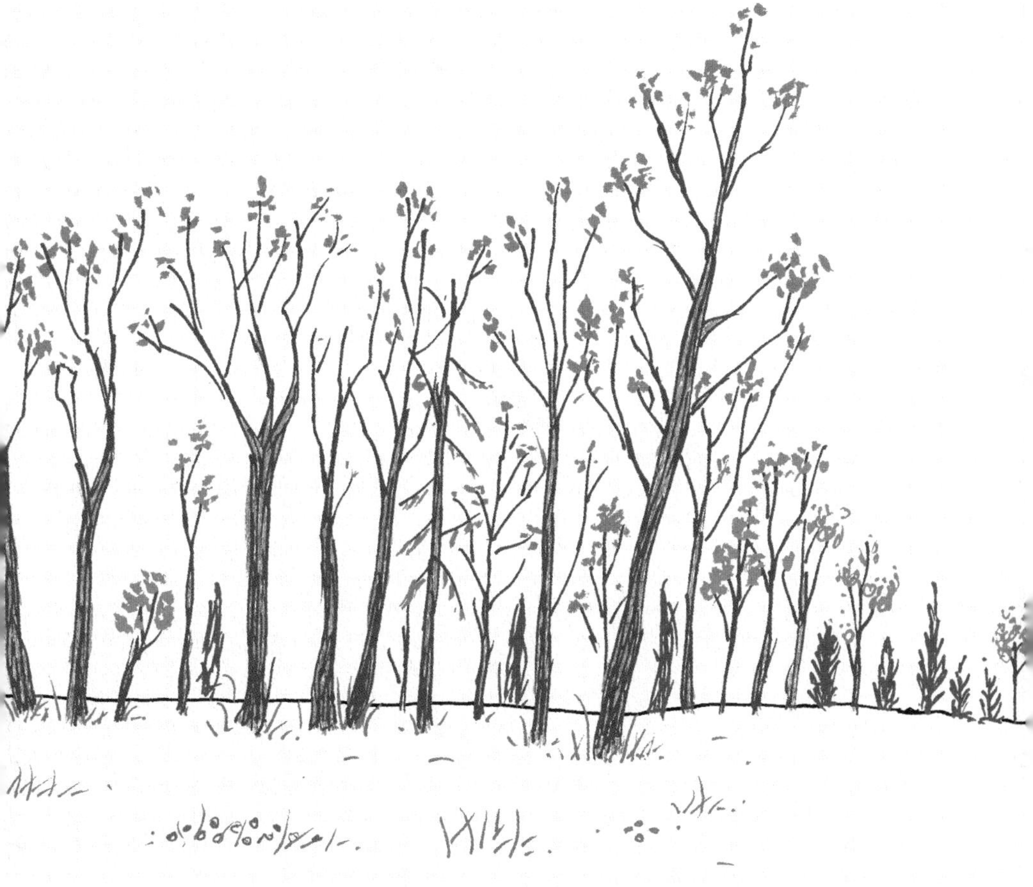

There are only two days in the year

that nothing can be done.

One is called **Yesterday,**

and the other is called **Tomorrow**.

Today is the right day to love, believe, do, and mostly live positively to help others.

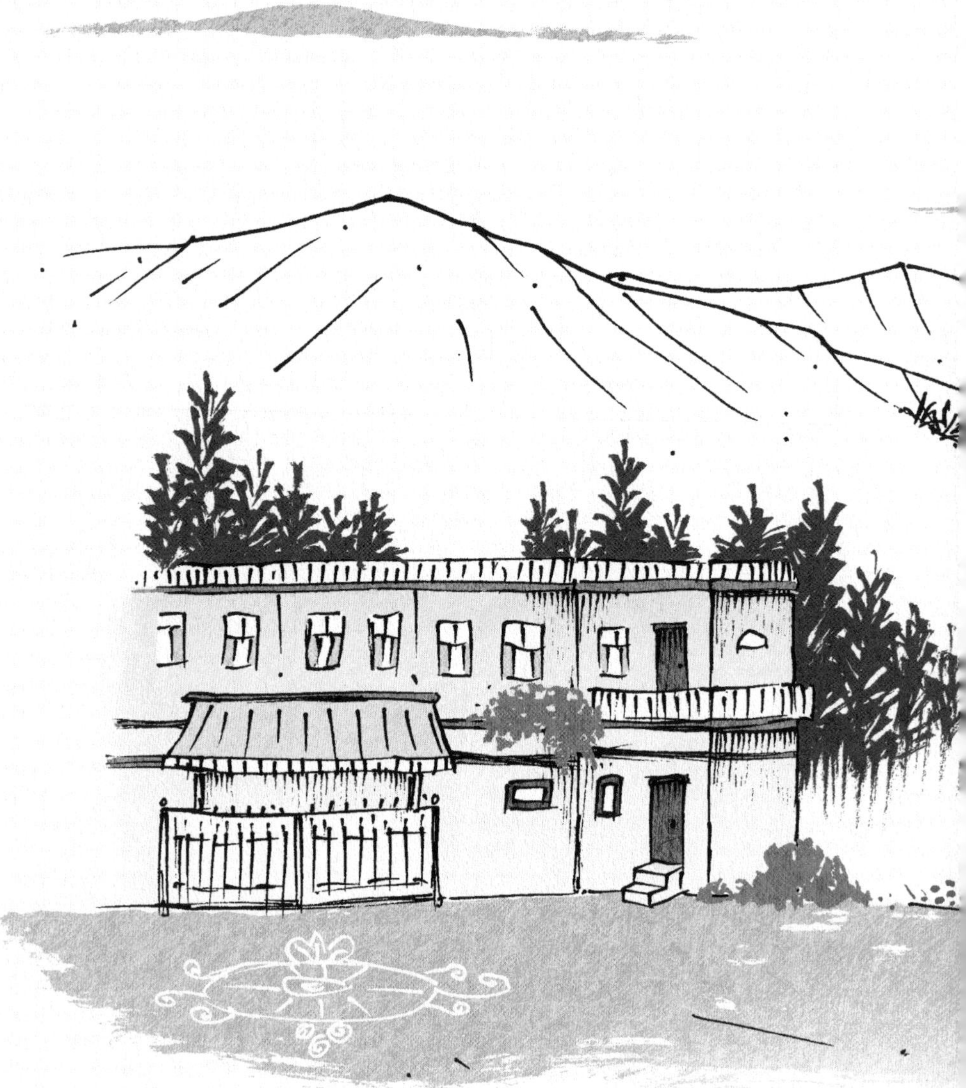

I pray for all of us,

that together we succeed

in building a compassionate world

through understanding and love,

and that in doing so

we may reduce the pain and suffering

of all sentient beings.

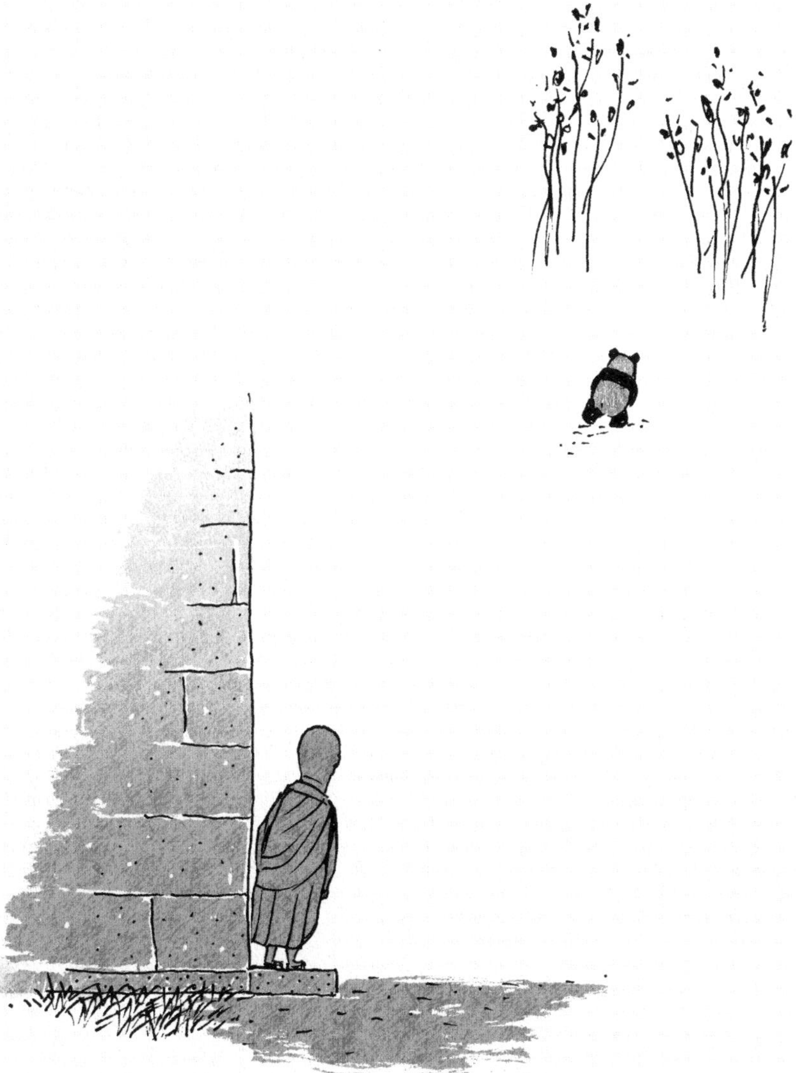

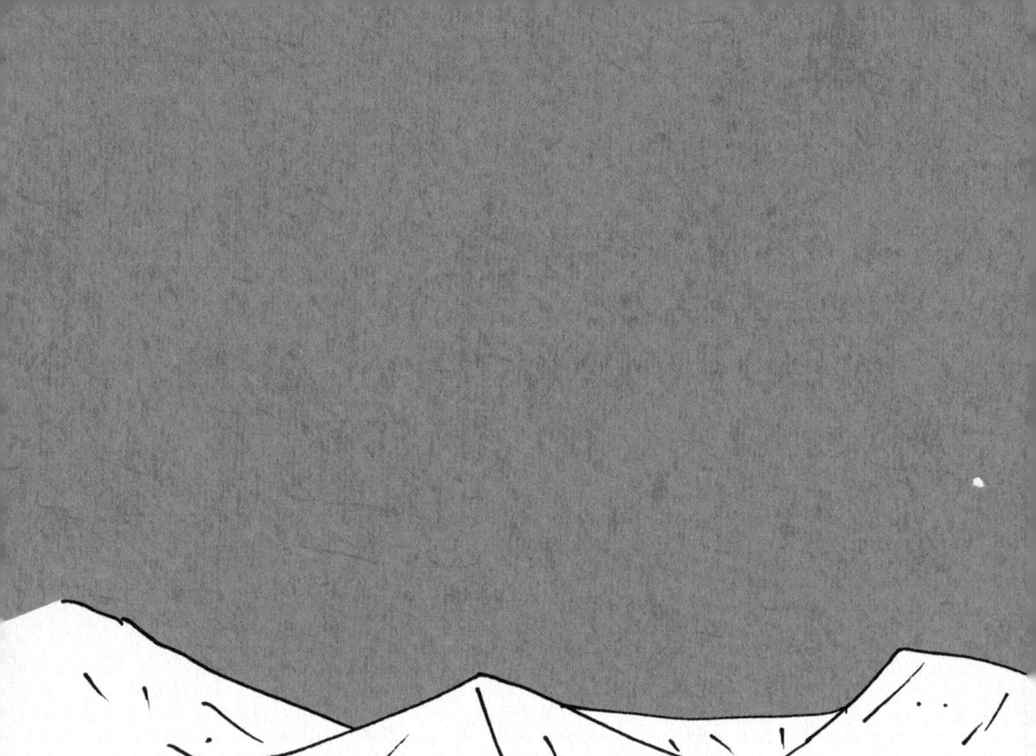

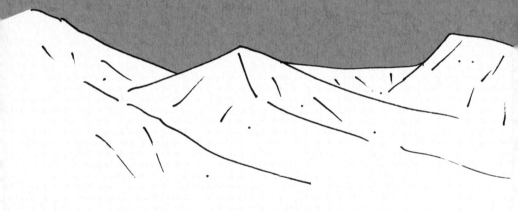

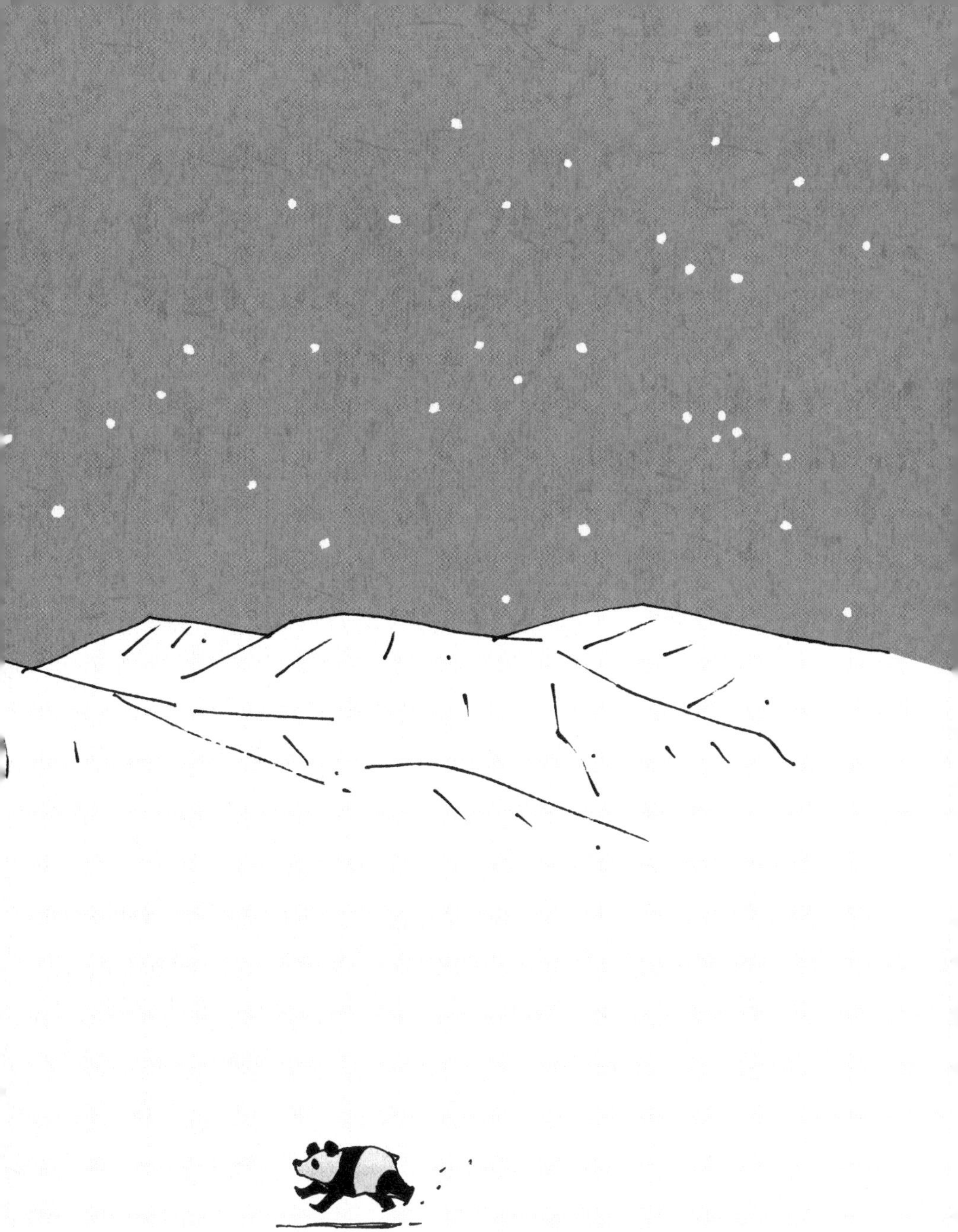

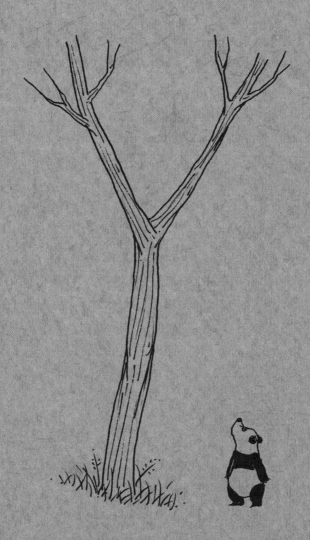

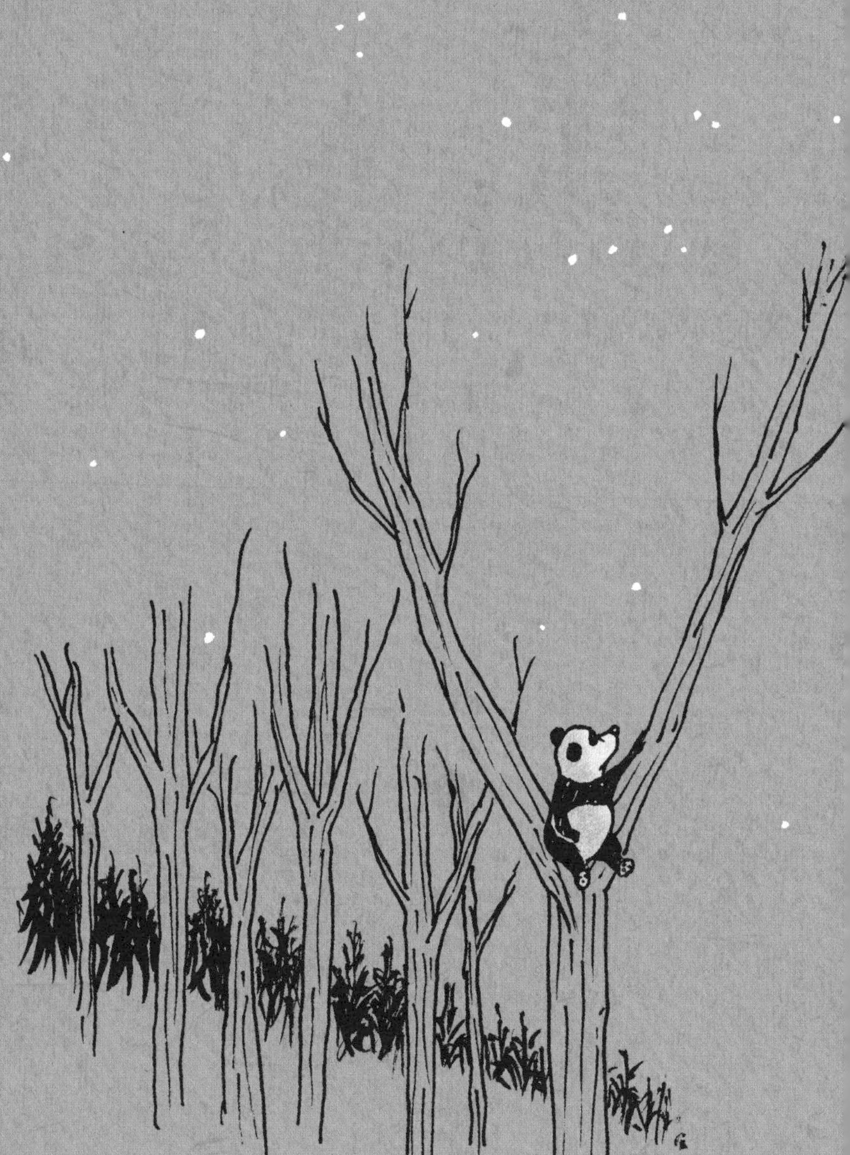

May I become at all times, both now and forever,

A protector for those without protection

A guide for those who have lost their way

A ship for those with oceans to cross

A bridge for those with rivers to cross

A sanctuary for those in danger

A lamp for those without light

A place of refuge for those who lack shelter

And a servant to all in need.

For as long as space endures,

And for as long as living beings remain,

Until then may I, too, abide

To dispel the misery of the world.

"KNOCK"

"KNOCK"

May all sentient beings,
oneself and others,
find constant happiness
through love and compassion
associated with wisdom.

THE DALAI LAMA

Every day, around the world, we see the devastating consequences of our disregard for this precious planet, our only home. Mother Earth is teaching us a lesson in the need for universal responsibility. We can no longer close our eyes and hope that what is happening in the natural world is not as serious as what many experts are predicting. We must all work to protect the fragility of the planet before it's too late.

The noble panda in this book is an innocent bear who faces great challenges. As the weather changes, he sees his habitat disappear and his species diminish. We witness these things, too. However, unlike the panda and other animals, we can do something about them.

It is my hope that this book will open the eyes, minds, and hearts of all people, particularly young people, to the importance of kindness and compassion toward our environment, on which we so depend for our survival.

His Holiness the Dalai Lama is the spiritual leader of Tibetan Buddhists. Born to a farming family in eastern Tibet on July 6, 1935, at the age of two he was recognized as the reincarnation of the thirteenth Dalai Lama, the spiritual and temporal leader of Tibet.

The Dalai Lama describes himself as a simple Buddhist monk. He often says, "I lost my freedom at sixteen and my country at twenty-four." Following the 1950 Communist Chinese invasion of Tibet, in March 1959 he escaped to India. Today he lives in Dharamsala, in the north Indian state of Himachal Pradesh.

The Dalai Lama travels the world spreading his message of peace, compassion, and the importance of recognizing the oneness of the seven billion human beings inhabiting our planet. To honor his nonviolent campaign to end the Chinese domination of Tibet, and for his ethical approach to countering climate change, he was awarded the Nobel Peace Prize in 1989.

In 2011, the Dalai Lama devolved his political authority to the elected leadership.

Environmental conservation is an essential principle of the Dalai Lama's in advocating universal responsibility. He emphasizes that each of us has a responsibility to ensure that the world will be safe for future generations—for our grandchildren as well as our great-grandchildren.

PATRICK MCDONNELL is the creator of the beloved comic strip *Mutts*, which has appeared in over 700 newspapers in 20 countries for over 25 years. Charles Schulz called *Mutts* "One of the best comics strips of all time." *Mutts* has received numerous awards both for its artistic excellence and for its animal- and environmental-protection themes.

McDonnell is the author of several *New York Times* bestselling picture books, including *The Gift of Nothing* and the Caldecott Honor–winning *Me . . . Jane* (a childhood biography of Jane Goodall). He has collaborated with spiritual teacher Eckhart Tolle on *Guardians of Being* and with poet/Rumi translator Daniel Ladinsky on *Darling, I Love You*.

∞

Patrick would like to thank His Holiness the Dalai Lama, Pam Cesak, Tencho Gyatso, Tseten Samdup Chhoekyapa, Judith Curr, Anna Paustenbach, Shawn Dahl, Robert McDonnell, Henry Dunow, Stu Rees, Karen O'Connell, and everyone who is doing their part to making the world a kinder, safer place for all beings.

Previously published material reprinted with permission:

Pages i, 36, 84: *My Tibet.* Copyright 1995 Text by His Holiness the Fourteenth Dalai Lama of Tibet. Used by permission from the University of California Press.

Pages 17, 23, 24, 41, 124, 131, 188, 189, 191: *Ethics for the New Millennium* by His Holiness the Dalai Lama. Copyright © 1999 by His Holiness the Dalai Lama. Used by permission of Riverhead, an imprint of Penguin Publishing Group, a division of Penguin Random House LLC. All rights reserved.

Pages 41, 52, 82, 84, 95, 99, 100, 107, 122: *Our Only Home: A Climate Appeal to the World.* © 2020 by His Holiness the Dalai Lama and Franz Alt. First published in the United States by Harlequin. Used by permission.

HarperCollins books may be purchased for educational, business, or sales promotional use. For information, please email the Special Markets Department at SPsales@harpercollins.com.

FIRST EDITION

Designed by Shawn Dahl, dahlimama inc

Library of Congress Cataloging-in-Publication Data has been applied for.

ISBN 978-0-06-321698-3

23 24 25 26 27 PNB 10 9 8 7 6 5 4 3 2 1

DalaiLama | DalaiLama | @DalaiLama | DalaiLama.com

MuttsComics | _PatrickMcDonnell | Mutts.com/HeartToHeart